# MICROMYSTERIES

*Stories of Scientific Detection*

# MICROMYSTERIES

## *Stories of Scientific Detection*

*Gail Kay Haines*

ILLUSTRATED WITH PHOTOGRAPHS



G. P. PUTNAM'S SONS · NEW YORK

*To my mother for her help and to my father, who always wants to find out how and why.*


Published in 1990 by G. P. Putnam's Sons, division of The Putnam & Grosset Book Group, 200 Madison Avenue, New York, NY 10016. Published simultaneously in Canada. Printed in the United States of America.

---

Library of Congress Cataloging-in-Publication Data
Haines, Gail Kay. Micromysteries. Reprint. Originally published: New York : Dodd, Mead, c1988. SUMMARY: Presents thirteen stories which describe how scientists used methods of microscopic investigation to uncover such mysteries as radioactivity, diabetes, microchips, and superconductors. 1. Science—Methodology—Juvenile literature. [1. Science—Methodology. 2. Scientists] I. Title. QC175.2.H3 1988b 500 89-70166 ISBN 0-399-61270-X 10 9 8 7 6 5 4 3 2

# CONTENTS

# 1

# THE STICKY SECRET

The original bumbling detective may have been Christopher Columbus. As the old story goes, when he set off he didn't know where he was going. When he landed, he didn't know where he was. When he got back, he didn't know where he had been, and he did it all on borrowed money.

In spite of that, Columbus discovered the Americas and helped solve a major mystery about the size and shape of the earth. Another bumbling detective, Charles Goodyear, faced even worse problems when he investigated a mysterious substance called rubber.

According to reports, when Columbus landed in Haiti he saw natives bouncing balls made from a strange elastic gum. Columbus (who thought he was in India) had never seen a material so odd. How could a ball hit the ground and then fly back into the air? He packed one of the mysterious toys to show his backer, Queen Isabella. He probably brought the first rubber to Europe.

The bouncing balls intrigued Columbus's crew, but riches—gold and jewels—interested them more. No one suspected that the strange gum might someday be valuable.

When Charles Goodyear entered the scene, more than three hundred years later, "India rubber"—the strange elastic gum from the New World—had become the latest craze. It stretched. It shed water. It could be made into waterproof shoes and wagon covers and whatever the customer needed. It looked like a quick path to riches.

But instead of quick riches, rubber plunged Goodyear into a nightmare of poverty, prison, and even near death. It led him straight into a major mystery.

Goodyear needed money. His family hardware business had failed, and frail, sickly Charles, thirty-four years old, owed almost everyone. A trip to New York, to borrow more money, failed too. Then Charles happened to glance into a New York shopwindow.

When Charles Goodyear stepped inside the Roxbury India Rubber Company store in spring, 1834, business was booming. Customers grabbed at the disappearing stacks of black rubber shoes and hats, wagon covers, and rubber-coated raincoats.

Too short to see over the crowd, Goodyear picked up a rubber life preserver from the window display. When he tried to blow it up, the valve stuck.

Instantly, Charles had a fabulous money-making idea. He would invent a better valve. He spent the last two dollars and fifty cents in his pocket to buy the rubber "doughnut," and he took it home to Philadelphia.

Weeks later, Goodyear walked back into the same store with

a new valve he had designed (much like the valve used in inflatable toys today). First, he sniffed. A terrible smell hung in the air.

Then he looked around, astonished. No eager shoppers, no merchandise! The store stood empty, except for the manager, handing out refunds to a couple of angry customers.

Stunned, Goodyear listened to the manager's list of miseries. Thirty thousand dollars worth of once-perfect shoes had been returned, melted by a summer heat wave into sticky black blobs. Everything else had melted, too. And everything stunk.

In fact, the warehouse reeked with the nauseating odor of disintegrating rubber. Many of the items smelled so bad that the company finally buried them in a deep pit near the factory.

In England, where the rubber industry started, summers are cool. Rubber products had lasted fairly well. But in the United States, rubber was turning into a disaster. In hot weather, it softened into a sticky mess. And in cold weather, rubber turned hard and brittle.

No one knew what to do. No one understood rubber's chemistry. Thousands of manufacturing dollars now hinged on a scientific mystery—how could rubber be controlled? The industry seemed sure to collapse unless someone found a solution.

Charles Goodyear couldn't sell his valve to a bankrupt company, but he loved hearing about the mystery. Rubber "is such a wonderful substance," he said. There had to be a way to handle it. Goodyear decided to turn his inventing talents to rubber.

Charles Goodyear came from a family of inventors. His father's steel pitchfork had revolutionized a farmhand's job, and patents on it and other inventions had been keeping his family fed since the store failed. Charles's own valve worked, even if the life preserver didn't.

Unfortunately, as soon as Goodyear stepped off the train, back home in Philadelphia, police arrested him. In those days, prison was the usual punishment for debt. Goodyear, with far more debts than money, had served time in debtor's prison before.

In fact, Goodyear had done some of his best inventing there. He already held patents for some farm machinery, a safe-eye metal button which would not fray thread, and a new type of faucet. Hours of the work had been done from a jail cell.

Now, from a new cell, he tackled the new project. In a little cottage on the prison grounds, Goodyear began chopping chunks of sticky, gummy rubber, mixing them with chemicals and rolling them out with his wife's rolling pin. Charles's wife, Clarissa, and one of the jailors kept him supplied with materials. Buying supplies wasn't easy, because Clarissa and their three children barely had enough money to eat.

Most American chemists favored turpentine for mixing with rubber. Fortunately, turpentine, used for thinning paint, was cheap. So was raw rubber. Charles mixed the pungent-smelling oil with tiny chunks of rubber and kneaded them into black "dough" with his hands. Then he worked in other chemicals to see what would happen. Finally, he rolled the mixtures out on a marble slab.

At first it looked easy. Goodyear, with no scientific training, discovered several different chemicals that could make rubber appear dry and smooth.

Then everything he had made started to sag out of shape. All his work melted into a sticky, decaying lump. Goodyear found himself back where he had started.

Selling a couple of old patents bought his way out of jail, and Goodyear began to work full time on the rubber mystery. For food and materials money, he pawned the furniture.

Next he tried kneading magnesia powder with sticky lumps of rubber. Mixing rubber with half its own weight of magnesia produced a smooth, white, dry surface. (Possibly Charles had the chemical on hand because he suffered from severe indigestion, then called "dyspepsia." Magnesia is a medication used to treat indigestion.)

Goodyear rolled out sheets of the mixture and made some into a waterproof book cover. It soon became soft and sticky.

Undaunted, he began coating cloth with the same mixture. Using $100 borrowed from an old friend, and with help from Clarissa and the children, he sewed rubber-coated fabric into hundreds of pairs of shoes. The Goodyears decorated them with bright patterns and colors, until they looked as elegant as any shoes in the shops. Goodyear stored them in a shed, as a test.

On the next really hot day, the shoes began to melt. The sticky mess soon smelled so foul that Charles had to bury it all.

The friend who had lent him that money refused to lend more, so Goodyear sold the rest of the furniture. Other friends advised him to give up and get a job.

Goodyear moved his family to a cheaper house and found a room in New York where he could experiment, rent-free. A druggist friend gave him the chemicals he needed. Without wasting time, Goodyear got back on the track of the mystery.

His next effort involved boiling a powdered chemical called

quicklime with rubber and turpentine. Smooth, unsticky sheets of rubber soon rolled off his marble slab. Goodyear saw success ahead. He quickly made up some articles to sell and even took out a patent "for a new discovery in India rubber."

Unfortunately, the results only "cured" the surface. Inside, rubber stayed as sticky as ever. And spilling an acid as mild as apple juice on the rubber could destroy the "curing" completely.

Since lime on the surface didn't work, Goodyear tried mixing quicklime throughout the rubber "dough." Lime is caustic to the touch. Kneading the sticky black mass as it cooled burned skin off his hands.

Then Goodyear found a small factory, three miles away, which would let him use some mixing equipment. He carried a large ball of rubber under his arm and a huge jar of lime on his shoulder, back and forth every day. Broke, as usual, he couldn't afford a horse and wagon.

Lime-treated rubber cloth looked gorgeous, and Goodyear thought of a special way to advertise his new product. He made himself an entire suit of rubber-coated clothes. "If you see a man who has on an India rubber cap, stock, coat, vest, and shoes, with an India rubber purse without a cent of money in it, that is I," Goodyear said about himself.

This time he thought for sure he had the mystery solved. Then his fancy rubber clothes began to fall apart. The burning effects of lime eventually destroyed the rubber. Another failure.

India rubber came from the milky juice of South American trees called cachuchu (spelling varies). The "India" part came from Columbus, and a British chemist named it "rubber" because he found it could rub out pencil marks better than the moist bread crumbs most people used. Rubber erasers once sold for as much as twenty dollars in today's money. But in Goodyear's time, "rubber" was fast becoming a synonym for "financial disaster."

Meanwhile, Charles already knew what to try next. Goodyear had used nitric acid to wash metallic paint off one of his decorated samples of rubber. The surface seemed to shrivel, and Goodyear threw it into the trash.

A few days later he dug it out, just in case it could be reused for something. Most of the sample stuck to his hands and to itself. But to Goodyear's amazement, the acid-washed spot felt smooth and dry. This looked like the best clue yet to the mystery.

Enthusiasm high, Goodyear plunged into experiments with acid and rubber. He took out another patent, for his new "acid-gas" process. The rubber sheets it produced looked fantastic—smooth and sleek and totally unsticky.

Goodyear began to sell some of the articles he made. He even earned enough money to bring his family to New York, into a better house, and to buy some new furniture.

The new process won Goodyear medals from a trade fair. It drew in new investors and earned Goodyear the use of an abandoned rubber factory. President Andrew Jackson praised it.

Then disaster struck. Goodyear, who never had any training in chemistry, mixed some unnamed acids and metallic salts together in a small, windowless room. Poisonous gas began to seep into the air. Before he knew what was happening, he had generated enough poison to knock himself unconscious.

Workmen found Charles, some time later, sprawled on the

laboratory floor. Goodyear hovered near death for days.

Strength of will and Clarissa's nursing helped Goodyear survive the deadly gas. He spent seven weeks in bed, recovering. As soon as he could sit up, Goodyear covered the bedspread with papers, plans, and sheets of rubber.

Charles didn't want to waste a minute, because he was certain this time he had to be right. And he did seem to be right. Thinner articles of acid-gas-treated rubber held their shape well, although thicker items still deteriorated in the first heat wave. He found a new backer and borrowed more money.

This time, a new disaster struck. The whole U.S. economy sagged. A general recession dried up sources of money, and Goodyear's backer went bankrupt. The factory had to close. Charles couldn't find anyone else willing to risk a cent on rubber.

Rubber had become a joke. People said it ought to be left where it came from, in the Amazon jungle, with the snakes and the headhunting natives. And people said Goodyear ought to give up and find a way to support his family. He lost the new house and had to move his wife and children into the factory. Soon he began pawning the new furniture.

More ups and downs over the next year landed Goodyear at a shut-down rubber plant in Woburn, Massachusetts. There, he uncovered a major clue to the rubber mystery.

Working almost alone at the abandoned factory, a British rubber worker, Nathaniel Hayward, tried a fresh idea. He mixed small amounts of a foul-smelling yellow chemical called sulfur, with his rubber. Then he dried it in the sun. According to his own first report, he used fumes of sulfur as a bleach. Instead of black, his rubber was almost white.

Hayward's rubber seemed to stay dry a little longer than Goodyear's efforts. Always scrupulously honest, Goodyear suggested that Haywood patent his "solarization" process. He did, and Goodyear bought the patent for three thousand dollars—of borrowed money.

Hayward could not even write his own name. He made "his mark" on a contract to work for Goodyear and to share "all his knowledge," for $800 a year. Goodyear took over the plant.

Goodyear decided if a little sulfur helped, a lot of sulfur should work even better. It did.

Combining sulfur with the acid-gas process, Goodyear and Hayward began making everything from life preservers to tents to ladies' cloaks out of rubber. Prosperity began to boom. At last the Goodyears could afford to redeem their furniture from the pawnshop.

For the first time in years, rubber began to get good publicity. Best of all, Goodyear was awarded a contract to produce 150 waterproof mailbags for the the U.S. Post Office out of sulfur and acid-treated rubber. The *Boston Post* predicted rubber would begin to replace other materials everywhere "should they succeed, as there can be but little doubt they will."

The Boston *Courier* called rubber "very durable," and free of "obnoxious smells." The publishers printed a few copies of the June 19, 1838, paper on rubber sheets Charles sent them.

But the whole future of rubber seemed to hinge on the mailbags. Could Goodyear finally deliver a perfect product? Was the mystery of rubber finally solved?

Charles and Clarissa worked for weeks to sew and decorate all the bags. Then they hung them in the shed.

The weather turned unusually hot. A few days later, an

awful odor seeped out from under the shed door.

Inside, the heavy bags had begun to ferment. Their painted surfaces still looked beautiful and smooth, but layers of uncured rubber underneath had begun to spoil.

A few weeks later most bags, hung by their handles, had sagged all the way to the floor. Everyone in town knew Goodyear had a contract with the Post Office and everyone in town knew he had failed to deliver. Again.

Customers started returning the ruined, foul-smelling life preservers and other rubber objects they had bought. The acid-gas-sulfur process still couldn't solve the mystery.

Unfortunately for Goodyear, the real problem took place deep inside the rubber. The real mystery of rubber involved its structure—molecules far too tiny to see.

Charles Goodyear did not even understand what he was trying to do. Rubber still baffled chemists all across the world. In 1838, they had no idea how complex a tiny molecule could be.

Natural rubber comes in long, skinny molecules made of thousands of chemical "units," linked together end-to-end, like a chain. Each unit is identical to the rest, combining five carbon and eight hydrogen atoms.

Modern chemists label rubber $(C_5H_8)_n$. The "n" stands for the number of units, or "links," usually from 4,000 to 5,000.

Goodyear's efforts to tame rubber didn't work because the chemicals he added always worked their way to the surface of the rubber. Inside, long (but far too small to see) chainlike molecules slithered around on top of each other, something like a pile of slippery snakes. Heat always made them slide apart and sag to the floor in a heap.

Meanwhile, Goodyear and Hayward had been ignoring a vital clue. Sulfur worked best on rubber dried in the sun. Neither man thought to try using heat. No one had ever used heat to cure rubber. As far as they knew, heat always destroyed rubber.

Stories differ on how Goodyear actually solved the mystery. His own account doesn't say exactly where it happened, but in January, 1839, somehow Goodyear accidentally dropped a chunk of sulfur-cured rubber on a hot stove.

Expecting a melted, smelly mess, he tried snatching the hot rubber off. To Goodyear's absolute amazement, the rubber had not melted the slightest bit. Rubber *always* melted under extreme heat! What could be happpening?

Goodyear examined the sample. Some parts had charred, almost like leather, but most of the piece felt smooth and elastic. In fact, it seemed stronger and more stable than any rubber he had ever touched. Heating the sulfur-cured rubber had made an amazing difference.

Goodyear shouted with excitement and showed everyone in the room his discovery. No one even paid attention. They had all heard it too many times before.

That night, Goodyear tacked the piece of sulfur and heat-cured rubber outside on the wall. Winter nights in Massachusetts are bitterly cold. But the next morning, his sample felt as smooth and elastic as before.

To test the change, he tried boiling pieces of rubber in hot sulphur-water, as hot as he could make it. The rubber should have melted, but it didn't. Strong, foul-smelling fumes of sulfur rolled off the kettle, but nothing affected the rubber. In fact, Goodyear could not get any sample of sulfur-treated rubber to melt, no matter how hard he tried.

Goodyear didn't know it, but inside the rubber, vital changes had taken place. He had finally hit on a chemical process that worked!

Atoms of sulfur, aided by heat, attached themselves to the individual links in rubber's long, chainlike molecules and then cross-linked the chains together. Instead of slithery snakes, the rubber now acted like a chainlink fence. It still had rubber's elastic "give," but now it always returned to its original shape. The cross-linking gave the tiny molecules no choice.

The inside of the rubber could no longer slither away. Without knowing how or why it had happened (chemists didn't figure it out for another hundred years), Goodyear had solved the mystery of rubber.

Naturally, life didn't get simple for the Goodyear family. Charles's amazing rubber cure, which came to be called *vulcanization*, turned out to be so simple that other inventors and manufacturers started using it without recognizing Goodyear's patent. Even Nathaniel Hayward changed his story and said the sulfur-and-heat idea had originally been his. He had seen it "in a dream," he told the court.

Money poured in, but lawsuits put Goodyear further in debt than ever. When the French general Napoleon awarded him a medal, Goodyear accepted it from jail. Money and medals never mattered as much to Charles Goodyear as solving the mystery he set out to solve. Today, vulcanization is still the process which cures natural and synthetic rubber for use in all kinds of tires and other rubber objects.

Charles Goodyear spent years chasing a mystery. He blundered upon the key. Once he solved the puzzle, he didn't understand what he had done, and, like Columbus, he did it all on borrowed money. And like Columbus, his discovery changed the world.

# 2

# THE MYSTERY OF THE EMPEROR'S NEW METAL

The problem had baffled the world's greatest chemists for more than fifty years. What could they do about aluminum?

An amazing new metallic element first isolated in 1825, aluminum had a beautiful silvery-white sheen, never rusted, and weighed less for its size than any other metal chemists knew about. Best of all, the shiny metal was quite abundant, found in rocks and clay and gemstones and just plain dirt all over the world.

Aluminum could be put to all sorts of uses, except for one mysterious difficulty—unlike gold or silver or copper, aluminum metal is never found pure in nature. It forms a strong attachment to other elements and does not easily let go. In the mid-1800s, pure aluminum cost more than gold.

Working in a chemistry laboratory at Oberlin College in Ohio, one day in 1885, Charles Martin Hall heard his professor state that the person who discovered a cheap way to purify aluminum would benefit the world and "be able to lay up for himself a great fortune."

"I'm going for that metal," Charles whispered to a classmate.

Charles loved a chemical mystery better than anything. Since he was sixteen, Charles had been hanging around the chemistry department at Oberlin, making friends with the professors, buying "a few cents worth of glass tubing or test tubes or something," and doing chemical experiments.

Now at twenty-two and about to graduate, he felt well prepared to tackle the mystery of aluminum. The trouble was, chemists all around the world had already tried and failed.

The first major scientist to take on aluminum was the famous English chemist Humphry Davy. Davy had isolated and purified several other metals by passing electricity through a vat of dissolved metallic chemicals. This procedure was called electrolysis, and shiny layers of pure metal always gathered at one of the battery connections, or electrodes. Davy decided to try his method on a new chemical discovery.

No one had seen it yet, but chemists believed a new metal lay hidden inside most rocks and certain chunks of ore. Davy was so sure his electrolysis procedure would uncover the hidden substance that he gave the new metal a name: aluminum. He set up his equipment and started the power. Unfortunately, nothing happened. No matter how carefully Humphry Davy did the experiment or how often he tinkered with the equipment, no aluminum appeared. Not even a trace.

Davy gave up. Aluminum did not behave the way other metals did. Aluminum was a mystery.

Other chemists, over the next few years, tried variations on the same technique. No luck. The mysterious metal held tightly to whatever it happened to be combined with. It wouldn't let go.

Finally, a Danish physicist, Hans Christian Oersted, found a way to chemically extract a few dusty gray granules of pure aluminum metal from solution. Chemists improved upon his method until they could finally produce, slowly and expensively, small, silvery-white bars of the pure, light metal.

The first part of the aluminum mystery—how to make it pure—had been solved. Unfortunately, the shiny new metal cost more than $545 a pound, in times when houses sold for less.

Jewelers turned sheets of aluminum into cuffs and bracelets and necklaces. The Emperor Napoleon III had an aluminum rattle designed for his baby, and he bought some aluminum forks and spoons, which he saved for his most honored guests. The rest had to eat with gold.

Napoleon ordered armor for a few favored soldiers made from the amazingly light metal, and a costly sheet of aluminum topped the just-built Washington Monument. Aluminum was a great hit as a toy for the wealthy, but not useful for much else. It simply cost too much.

By the time Charles Hall came on the scene, other chemists had worked the price down from $500 a pound to about $8 a pound, but that still put aluminum out of reach of most people. No one knew what to do next.

Except Charles Hall. He took his professor's remark about becoming rich and famous very seriously. He laid out some lab equipment and set out to solve the mystery, in his spare time.

Charles tried several chemical methods of extracting aluminum from its ore, filling the halls of the chemistry building with strong, poisonous fumes. Nothing worked. Finally, he decided to give electrolysis another try. Maybe he could succeed where the famous Humphry Davy—and others—had failed.

None of the batteries at Oberlin produced enough current. Charles and his favorite professor, Dr. F.F. Jewett, had to almost completely redesign them. Weeks of work finally paid off in strong batteries, but no aluminum.

Graduation gave the five-foot, eight-inch young man, who still "looked like a little boy," more spare time, but no laboratory to work in. Charles took his apparatus home and set up a workspace in his parents' woodshed, making some new equipment, including a small clay crucible, or dish, to hold his solutions. He borrowed the rest. Dr. Jewett loaned him a large handmade battery and a small gasoline stove for heating his products.

At home, Charles set up the same electrolysis experiment everyone else had already tried. Everyone else had always failed. So did Charles. Nothing happened. One reason was simple. A metal has to be in a liquid solution before electrolysis can work, and most compounds of aluminum are hard, insoluble chunks of rock.

Like other chemists before him, Charles managed to dissolve several compounds of aluminum. But when he connected the batteries and waited to see what would happen, water in the solution began breaking down. Bubbles of oxygen and hydrogen gas floated off at the electrodes. No shiny metal lumps appeared.

With most other metals, the metal deposits itself at an electrode before water has a chance to break down. Not aluminum. Aluminum's behavior was still a mystery.

Charles tried dozens of other solvents and solutions, with every kind of aluminum ore he could find. Everything failed. Was aluminum so unreactive it didn't move? All that electricity passing through had to be doing *something*. Again and again, he connected the batteries and then disconnected them in disappointment. Nothing!

No matter how much aluminum he managed to dissolve in his crucible, none appeared at the electrode. Not ever. He kept trying different things, collecting clue after clue to the mystery. Unfortunately, all the clues were negative. Charles now knew more than a hundred things which did not work.

From all that effort, Charles began to see how the chemistry of aluminum worked. Aluminum was not less reactive than silver and gold, it was more reactive. He could have guessed that already, from the way aluminum held on to other chemicals. Instead of moving through the solution toward an electrode, aluminum reacted right away. With water. Charles had uncovered the first useful clue.

Now Charles knew what he had to do next. The water had to go—every single drop of it. But how? All of the chemicals he used to dissolve his aluminum ore were partly water.

Then a brilliant new idea occurred to Charles. What if he tried melting his compounds? Or at least, melting some water-free chemical to use as a solvent. He began to look for a special kind of solvent, one which would melt first and then dissolve powdered aluminum ore in the resulting hot liquid.

Using his chemical knowledge, Charles decided that a compound of the element fluorine ought be the best, because fluorine is the most chemically active element of all. Surely it could pull aluminum out of its rocky hiding places.

He ground calcium fluoride ore into small chunks, heated his homemade crucible to as high a temperature as possible, and watched to see what would happen. Nothing happened. His ground-up rocks just sat there.

The heat needed to melt most kinds of aluminum ore is far higher than Charles could possibly have produced. Fortunately, Charles didn't know he was trying to do the impossible.

Charles tried all the easy-to-get fluoride compounds first. None of the compounds he tried worked. Either they wouldn't melt, like magnesium and aluminum fluoride, or, like sodium or potassium fluoride, they wouldn't dissolve any ore. Charles kept trying.

Charles began experimenting with more exotic kinds of fluoride crystals. Dr. Jewett let him search through the resources of the chemistry department at Oberlin, borrowing what he needed.

Finally, Charles picked up a container of sodium aluminum fluoride, or cryolite, a rare translucent mineral found mainly in Greenland. He ground the colorless crystals into a fine, white powder, which melted easily. So far, so good, but he had been disappointed before.

Now for the next step. Charles stirred in some gritty granules of another mineral called alumina. To his amazement, it dissolved almost instantly. He added more. It also dissolved.

Charles knew any stray water would already have boiled away. The melted cryolite solution registered a temperature much higher than boiling water. He was ready to try electrolysis again, except for a new problem: no battery. Charles had returned the borrowed battery to Dr. Jewett.

Charles hurried down the street to Oberlin College to borrow it again. He settled the two copper electrodes in the molten solution and turned on the current. Gas began to bubble, but nothing else happened. No aluminum.

This time, Charles had been so sure. He was still sure. Something must be stopping the aluminum again, before it could travel to an electrode. If not water, then something else. Some small problem still stood between him and fame and fortune. But what?

Charles stared at his mostly homemade equipment. The roughly shaped crucible was baked from clay, and clay is mostly the element silicon. Next to water and oxygen, aluminum likes best to combine with silicon. That's why the two make up so many different kinds of rock.

Charles guessed silicon had to be leaching out of his clay crucible and into solution, where it reacted with the aluminum. At least, he couldn't think of any other answer. He was back in the same mess as before.

But this time the solution came more easily. Charles built a new crucible, with one small improvement. This one he lined inside with black, unreactive carbon (similar to pencil lead). To be extra sure, he removed the copper electrodes from his battery and replaced them with carbon. Charles didn't want any more "small problems."

First thing in the morning, February 23, 1886, Charles started the whole experiment over. He melted some cryolite and added a small scoop of alumina. When it had fully dissolved, he carefully slid in the electrodes and turned on the current.

Now came the hardest part. He waited several hours. Something was happening inside the bubbling crucible, but

Charles couldn't tell what. Finally, he poured the thick molten mess into an old iron skillet borrowed from his mother.

Charles didn't wait for the solution to cool. As soon as the cryolite solidified, and while it was still too hot to touch, Charles dumped it out and smashed the whole chunk with a hammer. It shattered into chalky bits, leaving some small, silvery "buttons" of pure aluminum on the table.

The method worked, and the mystery was almost solved. That same morning, Charles raced back to Oberlin with the buttons clutched in the palm of his hand. "Professor, I've got it," he announced to Dr. Jewett.

Fame and riches didn't come immediately. It took Charles a few years to get enough backing and set up a company to mass-produce aluminum. And it took a while for the public to learn what to do with all that cheap aluminum. Within a few decades, aluminum was being used for everything from automobile parts and aircraft to foil candy wrappers.

Part of Charles Hall's problems in selling his process for making aluminum came from an amazing coincidence. A young French chemist, born the same year as Charles, 1863, had independently discovered almost exactly the same process for making aluminum. Paul Louis Toussaint Hérault was selling his method all over Europe.

The two finally worked out the financial details, and their method, still in use today, is often called the Hall-Hérault process. As a final coincidence, Hérault died in 1914, the same year as Charles Hall.

Charles Martin Hall received the Perkin Medal in 1911, for excellence in chemistry. When he died, he left $5 million, a third of his wealth, to Oberlin College.

# 3

# THE SECRET IN THE OLD SHED

The mysterious rays first turned up when Henri Becquerel decided to investigate X-rays. The time: February, 1895. The place: Paris, France.

X-rays became an overnight sensation. Discovered in Germany by Wilhelm Roentgen, the strange, invisible beams of energy could pass right through living flesh. Within days of the famous discovery, doctors everywhere began taking pictures of their patients' bones.

Scientists all over the world tripped over each other trying to be the first to solve the mystery of the strange, penetrating X-rays, generated by passing electricity through a glass vacuum tube. In France, physicist Antoine Henri Becquerel thought he had a great new clue.

Becquerel knew certain crystals glow in the dark after exposure to sunlight. He noticed that the same crystals, called phosphorescent, also glow when X-rays hit them.

The glowing crystals must be giving off some kind of

mysterious rays of their own. Could those feeble lights be a weaker kind of X-ray? Henri decided to find out.

X-rays penetrate flesh and skin. Phosphorescent rays don't. Becquerel wanted to see if his rays were strong enough to penetrate something easier. He chose paper.

Henri tried several glow-in-the-dark compounds made of zinc and calcium, exposing them to the sun as they lay on carefully wrapped photographic plates. Sunlight couldn't get through the thick black wrapping paper. He had already checked that. Could the phosphorescence penetrate the paper?

If so, it would fog the plate. He developed each photographic plate carefully. Nothing! No sign of fog. The negatives showed a total white blank.

Then Becquerel remembered some phosphorescent uranium salts he had loaned to a friend. Shaped and polished into disks, the beautiful crystals gave off an extra-strong glow after exposure to the sun. Maybe they would work better.

The morning his colleague returned Becquerel's crystals, a winter sun shone brightly over Paris. Becquerel immediately set up the experiment.

He wrapped a photographic plate in two sheets of heavy black paper, put a flat disk of uranium salt on top, and exposed the whole thing to the sun for several hours. Then he developed the plate.

A dark, mysterious shadow appeared. In Becquerel's words, he saw "the silhouette of the phosphorescent substance, appearing in black on the negative."

Success! Thinking he had discovered a "new" kind of X-ray, Becquerel tried the same experiment several more times. It always worked. If he placed a small coin under the sample, the coin's image showed up clearly in white, inside the disk's black shadow.

Becquerel reported his findings to the French Academy of Science. No one paid much attention. Phosphorescent rays didn't sound very mysterious. Or very interesting. Becquerel decided to try for better "pictures."

Heavy clouds hung over Paris for the next several days. Becquerel set his uranium sample on a small copper cross, both atop a paper-covered photographic plate. He laid the whole thing neatly inside a drawer, waiting for the sun to shine. It stayed there all week.

In those days, scientists rarely worked on Sunday. But the Academy met every Monday, and Becquerel may have wanted something new to report. Maybe he had a hunch.

Or perhaps he just wanted to demonstrate his technique to a visiting friend. Whatever the reason, Becquerel decided on Sunday, March 1, 1896, to develop the plate in the drawer.

To his absolute astonishment, Becquerel saw that the negative—which should have been nearly blank—showed a darker image than ever. Becquerel *fut stupéfait* (was stupefied), said his eighteen-year-old son, Jean.

Becquerel's friend Sir William Crookes happened to be visiting that day. Crookes described the plate as "darkened strongly," with "the image of the copper cross shining out white against the black background." An unbelievable effect from a nonglowing phosphorescent sample.

Becquerel soon learned, to his growing amazement, that his crystals didn't need to be glowing. They didn't need exposure to the sun at all. A sample of uranium salt could take its own picture anytime, even after months in the dark.

Every compound of uranium, not just phosphorescent ones, showed the same mysterious effect. A chunk of pure uranium metal made the clearest image of all.

Becquerel brought uranium samples close to an electrometer, a device used to measure electricity. He discovered that uranium actually electrifies the air around it. Invisible energy seemed to be pouring out of uranium, all by itself.

Becquerel realized his discovery had nothing to do with phosphorescence and nothing to do with X-rays. Henri Becquerel had uncovered a new mystery. "Rayons uraniques," as Becquerel named them, had a mystical power all their own. But how? And why? He didn't have a clue.

Later, in another part of Paris, Marie Curie began searching for a good mystery to solve. She had already earned degrees in mathematics and physics, but she wanted what no woman had ever achieved before—a doctorate in science. It would take a miracle! Or maybe, it would take a research project so outstanding that all the male professors would be forced to notice.

Marie combed the scientific literature, looking for the perfect subject for her thesis. Something original. Something important. Something—unusual. She found it, in Becquerel's mysterious discovery.

No one else seemed to be working on the uranium puzzle. Even Becquerel had moved on to other things. Marie made up her mind to solve the mystery of the invisible rays.

In 1897, women scientists did not have easy access to laboratories, not even if they happened to be married to physics professors. After weeks of effort, Pierre Curie, Marie's husband, found her a spot. He got permission for Marie to work in a glass-walled storeroom at the School of Physics and Chemistry, where he taught.

Cast-off equipment and stacks of lumber littered the cold, damp room. Marie didn't mind. She moved her materials in right away, and by January, 1898, her mystery-solving project took off.

She wrote out a plan of action. Becquerel had already shown that uranium salts cause the air around them to conduct electricity. Marie planned to measure that electricity precisely.

Her makeshift lab was almost bare of equipment, but here Marie got a lucky break. Pierre and his brother Jacques, also a physicist, had already invented the perfect instrument for this very delicate job—a special electricity-measuring device called a piezoelectrique-quartz electrometer.

Crystals under pressure give off a small electric current. (Pierre was the first to discover the fact.) A piezoelectrique-quartz electrometer measures electricity by balancing the energy released from a crystal of quartz under pressure against the current given off by the sample being measured.

Pierre loaned Marie his own electrometer. He helped her set it up in her new "lab." One flat metal plate held the sample, while another plate absorbed the current.

An electrometer needs an unchanging temperature and low humidity to work properly. In her lab, in January, the temperature usually varied from cold to freezing. As for humidity, moisture condensed on the glass walls and dripped from the high ceiling.

Marie shielded her instruments as well as she could. She began to make precise measurements of the intensity of the electrical current caused by different compounds of uranium.

Clue #1 turned up quickly. Marie found that each sample of uranium salt, as well as uranium metal itself, charged the electrometer a definite amount, based upon how much uranium the sample contained. Repeated experiments produced the same results.

Next, Marie tried to see if she could alter those results. She heated the crystals. No change. She carefully dried all the water out of her samples. Still no change.

Marie ground crystals to a fine powder, dissolved them, and combined them with other chemicals. Nothing she did made the slightest difference. A weighed sample of any uranium compound continued to produce exactly the same amount of current, no matter what Marie did to it.

Madame Curie ran the same experiments over and over, with fresh samples of each compound. Thoroughness was her scientific method. She had an obsession about getting things right.

Through the coldest part of winter, Marie spent almost every day in the barely heated study. Then every evening she hurried home to cook dinner for Pierre and herself, Pierre's father, and their baby, Irene.

Born in Poland, Manya Sklodovska, like her whole family, loved learning—from languages (she spoke five) to literature to sociology. But a chance to work evenings and weekends in a small laboratory directed by one of her cousins drove other ideas out of her head. She acquired, she said, "the taste for experimental research." Manya decided to become a physicist.

As soon as she earned enough money, Manya, with an assortment of baggage and a sack of caramels, took a train to

France. She enrolled at the Sorbonne, in Paris. In four cold, difficult years, living in a sixth-floor attic, she managed to earn two degrees and fall in love.

Pierre Curie, professor of physics, was intelligent, diligent, hard-working. He was also forgetful, unambitious, and completely uninterested in money. They married in July, 1895, the same year Roentgen discovered X-rays. Manya began calling herself "Marie," to go with her new French name.

When a relative gave Marie money for a wedding trousseau she used it, instead, to buy the only wild and frivolous purchase she probably ever made in her life—two bicycles, the year's biggest fad.

Marie and Pierre took long summer bicycle trips, riding all over the French countryside. The rest of the time, they worked.

Pierre's father moved in with them about the time their first baby was born, making it easier for Marie (who had the same problems working mothers have today) to get everything done. Three months later, Marie got started on the mystery.

Clue #2 was now clear. Nothing, neither physical nor chemical changes, could alter the radiation pouring out of uranium. Whatever the radiation was, Marie realized, it had to be coming from inside the uranium atoms themselves. This single fact turned out to be Madame Curie's greatest discovery.

Next, Marie needed to find out if this mysterious phenomenon happened only with uranium. Maybe other elements had the same property. She needed new samples to test.

Marie walked or bicycled around to all the scientific schools and laboratories she could reach, borrowing every salt and metal available. Marie searched until she had at least one sample of *every known chemical element.* Scientists knew about more than fifty elements in 1898, and Marie collected well over one hundred samples in all.

Meticulously, Marie placed a thin layer of each material, one at a time, on the metal plate of her electrometer, to see if any electrical charge surged toward the other plate. Mostly nothing happened.

Finally, Marie spotted what she had been hoping to find—more mysterious rays. A compound containing a metal called thorium charged the electrometer, just as uranium did.

Marie located other samples of thorium. Every one caused a current.

No other element had any effect on the electrometer. Marie had discovered clue #3. Two rare metals had something in common that no other known element had. They each gave off invisible, powerful rays.

Now, the mysterious rays needed a new name. "Rayons uraniques" no longer worked. Thorium had them, too. In a paper written for the Academy, Marie renamed them "Becquerel's rays." She also coined a new word to describe the invisible rays. Marie Curie called them "radioactivity."

So far, Marie had been testing salts and other pure chemicals. She had also measured the radioactivity of the two metals in their pure form. Now she wanted to test natural mixtures—ores and minerals and rocks.

The School of Physics had a mineral collection. Pierre helped Marie select the best samples. The Curies poured over crumbly rock fragments, grinding some of them into powders fine enough to spread across the electrometer's pan.

Again, Marie knew what she expected to find. Ores which had no uranium or thorium would show no activity. Ores which did, would.

Marie cleared all the inactive rocks and minerals out of her way first and began to concentrate on the few that were left. The next step in her plan called for making exact measurements on the radioactive ores and minerals she had uncovered. She expected, as before, to find that the amount of electric charge depended upon the amount of uranium or thorium inside.

To her amazement a few uranium ores, especially two called pitchblende and chalcolite, turned out to be much more active than she expected. Unbelievably, pitchblende seemed to be *four times* as radioactive as uranium!

The results didn't make sense. Maybe the instruments had broken down. Maybe she had weighed the samples wrong.

She redid her experiments again and again, some as many as twenty times. She always got the same puzzling results. Marie hadn't just discovered a fresh clue, she had uncovered another mystery! Where could all that extra radiation be coming from?

Marie Curie had a very good idea what the solution to this new mystery would be. Only a hidden "something" inside the ore—something so strongly radioactive that a tiny trace of it could cause measurable activity—fit all the facts.

Marie had already examined every known element. The tiny "something" hidden inside her ore could only be a new, completely unsuspected element, present in such unbelievably small quantities that no one had ever spotted it before.

No one but Pierre believed her. Other physicist friends advised the Curies to be very careful before they made any embarrassing wrong announcements.

Marie ignored the advice. She wrote a paper announcing the "probable presence" of a new element, "endowed with powerful radioactivity." A former teacher presented Marie's paper to the Academy. (She and Pierre were not members.) Few scientists took it seriously.

"We are sure," she wrote to her sister Bronya. "The element is there, and I've got to find it." Just as Becquerel had abandoned X-rays to investigate uranium, Marie now abandoned uranium to search for the mysterious new element.

The young physicist had wanted to prove her theory "as rapidly as possible." For the first time, she began to need help. She needed Pierre.

So far, Pierre had given only occasional advice and some assistance in getting materials. Now, he put away his own research on crystal growth and joined Marie as an equal partner in the damp, cluttered workroom. They tackled the new mystery together.

The situation looked formidable. Pitchblende had been thoroughly studied by chemists already, and no one had seen any hints of unknown, mystery elements. The amount must be too small to detect, except by its radioactivity.

Guessing, they predicted about one percent of pitchblende might be their mystery element. One part in a hundred. Not much to work with, when the total amount of the expensive ore they possessed could be held in one hand. They started with a 100-gram sample, about the weight of 33 pennies, hoping to find a one-gram solution to the mystery.

Guessing, the Curies made a lucky error. The actual quantity of their "mystery element" in pitchblende is closer to one part in a million, or about one ten-thousandth of a gram of their original sample. If they had known that, they might never have started.

First, Marie and Pierre ground their small sample to a fine black powder and dissolved it in acid. Marie wrote down the date and data in one of her tiny black notebooks. (In another notebook, the same week, she noted, "Irene is showing her seventh tooth." In still another, she recorded the price of stockings and bicycle tires. Marie loved keeping records.)

Neither Curie was a chemist, but Marie taught herself the skills she needed. The Curies followed a regular chemist's scheme designed to separate pitchblende into all its different elements. They dissolved and filtered solutions, dried them, redissolved them.

Right away, clue #1 surfaced. At every separation, part of the product was radioactive and part was not. Each time, they threw away the nonradiating half.

"It was," wrote Marie's younger daughter, Eve, years later, "exactly the technique used by police when they search the houses of a neighborhood, one by one, to isolate and arrest a malefactor."

The size of their meager sample shrunk fast, but its radioactivity grew stronger. They were closing in on the mystery.

June came. The workroom turned stifling hot. Only one small glass flask held what was left of their sample—mostly a colorless compound called bismuth nitrate. Marie knew her mystery element was hidden inside. It *had* to be. It had been "following" bismuth through the processes, the way chemically similar elements often do.

Carefully, she bubbled in hydrogen sulfide gas, ignoring its poisonous rotten-egg smell. A brownish-black solid precipitated, falling to the bottom of the flask. Part of it was bismuth, but not all.

Marie hoped her mystery element would precipitate faster than bismuth. Hopefully, it would fall to the bottom first.

She dried the black solid and measured it with her electrometer. With a flourish of excitement, she wrote the results in her notebook in large, underlined letters: "150 times more active than uranium."

The same day, Pierre took a tiny scoop of the dark solid and heated it in a test tube. A miniscule amount of black powder, blacker than the rest of the solid, began "climbing" the wall of the test tube.

He kept heating it until the tube cracked. When the broken glass had cooled, he scraped a few particles of the black powder onto clean glass and measured it with the electrometer. The tiny black specks measured 330 times the radioactivity of uranium!

Redissolving and reprecipitating their sample again and again, to get rid of as much bismuth as possible, the Curies finally held up a few blackish grains. Marie and Pierre Curie had discovered a new element. Marie named it "polonium," after the country where she was born.

It should have been the end, but it wasn't. For one thing, chemists were not willing to accept a few specks of black powder as a genuine new element. They wanted enough to see and test. Nothing but the powder's radioactivity pointed to a new element.

More importantly, the mystery wasn't over yet. In fact, another new one had developed.

The tiny sample of polonium definitely represented a new

element, all right. Marie was positive.

But what about the solution it precipitated from? When Marie checked, she discovered, to her surprise, that the leftover yellowish solution, after all the polonium was gone, still gave off mystery rays. In fact, it gave off even more rays than polonium did!

According to the chemical flow chart, nothing important should be left in the solution. Carefully, Marie rechecked for leftover uranium or polonium. Her chemial tests showed nothing. Nothing but chalky salts of a silvery-white metal called barium.

Marie knew barium was not radioactive. She had tested it already. Something had to be "following" barium through the steps of the chemical separations, the way polonium had "followed" bismuth. Something radioactive. Something *very* radioactive.

Another radioactive element had to be hiding inside what was left of the pitchblende. Marie had uncovered one more mystery!

Both Curies had been dragging with fatigue for weeks. Marie's fingers were so sore and cracked she could hardly move them. They needed a break. In late summer, almost all of Paris took a vacation. Marie and Pierre packed up Irene and bicycled away for a holiday in the country. The new mystery would have to wait.

Before she left, Marie made gooseberry jam. Her fingers carried so much radiation that the cookbook, tested years later, made radiation counters crackle. So did all her lab notes and even the furniture.

(Both Curies suffered from what scientists today call *radiation sickness*, which means damage to the body caused by exposure to intense radioactivity. The "bare hands" experiments they did would not be allowed today. Even work with materials much less radioactive than polonium and Marie's second "mystery element" is always done from behind shields, using remote control devices.)

In the fall, the Curies returned to the glass-walled studio. Gustave Bemont, a red-bearded chemist at the school, had joined their working team.

The new mystery substance, "the other," as Marie called it, seemed to be more soluble in water than uranium. It seemed to follow barium through every chemical process. It needed a name. Marie decided to name the new element "radium."

Barium is a soft metal related to calcium. Radium must be related to both. For months, Marie looked for something that made them different—something she could use to separate each element from the other.

She dried her tiny sample and redissolved it in sulfuric acid. Finally, something different happened. Only part of the colorless barium crystals dissolved, but all the radioactivity went into the solution.

Marie wrote an excited note in her little black book. Radium sulfate dissolved in the acid better than barium sulfate did. This might be the final clue.

Marie did the same step over and over, each time removing the undissolved barium. Each time, her sample's radioactivity got stronger.

Finally, it was radiating at a strength 900 times greater than pure uranium. It still wasn't pure, but it was the best she could do with the few tiny, colorless crystals she had left.

The Curies had found their second mystery element, radium, an element so much more radioactive than uranium or thorium or polonium that it seemed almost impossible to believe.

And in fact, most scientists did not believe it. Marie had only a colorless speck in a test tube. Most chemists wanted better proof.

Pierre wrote letters all over the world, searching for inexpensive sources of pitchblende. This time, they didn't need a cupful. They needed a mountainful, and they had no money to pay for it, even if they knew where to find it.

Then their luck changed. Pitchblende, mined in the hills of the Austrian empire, was valuable only for uranium to use in pottery dyes. After they removed the uranium, the owners simply dumped the leftover ore in a pile in the forest.

Through a friend, Pierre arranged to get a ton of the highly radioactive ore delivered to Paris, for just the shipping charges. That took almost every penny the two physicists had.

When sacks of the ugly brown dust arrived, delivery men dumped them in the courtyard outside their studio. Marie untied the first sack and ran her hands through the dirtlike ore, mixed with pine needles. Now, proof of her solution to the mystery looked possible.

Once again, the Curies again had no place to work. The scientists' delicate electrometers could not stand the smelly, poisonous gases the new, large-scale experiments would give off.

Across the courtyard from Marie's workroom stood an abandoned shed. Years before, the medical school had dissected cadavers (dead bodies) on the old pine tables inside. Now, the roof leaked puddles of rainwater onto a bare asphalt floor. At least, it was convenient to their first workroom, and to the sacks of ore piled outside.

Marie called it a "miserable shed," but as soon as Pierre got the necessary permission, they moved right in. The shed contained a few bare tables, a blackboard, and a stove with a rusty pipe. One famous chemist later called the workroom "a cross between a stable and a potato cellar."

It took four years of backbreaking work to sift out the radium hidden inside four *tons* of ore. All that effort and material yielded about a teaspoonful of pure silvery radium, which glowed "like faint, fairy lights." Marie considered every minute of work to be worthwhile. Radium, she said, was as much her "baby" as Irene.

The discovery of radium heaped honors upon both the Curies. Pierre was finally accepted into the prestigious Academy of Sciences. The Academy awarded "some prizes" to Marie.

Pierre got a professorship at the Sorbonne. Marie took a job teaching in a high school for girls. The scientific community just wasn't ready for women, even brilliant ones.

Marie didn't mind too much being snubbed. Her precious doctorate, which she finally received from the Sorbonne, meant much more to her.

In 1903, Marie and Pierre Curie and Henri Becquerel shared a Nobel Prize in Physics for the discovery and basic research into radioactivity. In 1911, after Pierre's accidental death, Marie won a second Nobel Prize, in Chemistry, for the discovery of radium. After Pierre's death, Marie was, to the amazement of almost everyone, given his professorship at the Sorbonne.

The discoveries Marie Curie made provide a background for

everything learned about radioactivity since. In an old, abandoned shed, she solved what has been called "the scientific mystery of the century."

# 4

# THE MYSTERY OF THE DEADLY DOTS

Spots and dots, delirium and death. The disease was a killer, attacking cowboys and range riders with a special vengeance. Mysteriously, one certain river valley in Montana seemed to be the focus of the spotted horror.

Shoshone Indians avoided Bitter Root Valley, named for the pink-flowered plant they collected as a medicine. The tribe thought evil spirits haunted the valley in springtime. Squaws sent there to gather firewood often developed chills and fevers, aching bones, and spots on their wrists and ankles. Most of the time, they died.

Nez Percé and Flathead Indians feared traveling through the area in the spring and early summer. Spring always brought a new round of the spotted death.

Settlers who moved into Bitter Root Valley with their cattle and horses often died, too, of the same deadly disease. Rocky Mountain spotted fever threatened anyone who dared venture into the "haunted" valley or the mountain foothills nearby. No one knew why.

Almost everyone had an idea about the mysterious "black measles." Indians blamed spirits—in the shape of gophers. Some mountaineers thought it might come from eating melted snow. Some farmers thought exposure to wet, cold spring weather might cause the sickness. A few people blamed the deadly spotted fever on ticks. The Rocky Mountain hills and valleys swarmed in spring with tiny ticks.

By 1901, the terrified settlers knew they needed help. Rocky Mountain spotted fever had become epidemic not just in the Bitter Root Valley and surrounding hills, but spreading into a wider, two-state area. They asked the governor of Montana to do something about the mysterious killer.

1902: Two hired Minnesota doctors started research. They thought they found a tiny one-celled parasite hiding in the victims' muscle tissue. It looked like the tick-carried parasite which causes Texas fever in cattle. No one could confirm the team's findings, and the Montana Board of Health ran out of funds to pay them. They went back home.

1903: A local doctor treated seven spotted fever victims who had all been bitten by ticks. He saw that as proof: ticks carry the deadly disease. Other doctors disagreed. They said they didn't always find bite marks on their patients. Anyway, *everyone* had tick bites, didn't they? Ticks were everywhere.

Real estate agents and land developers loudly opposed the tick theory. Who would buy tick-infested farmland if they thought the tiny bugs might be deadly? They got a U.S. Department of Agriculture insect specialist to argue in their favor.

1903: A doctor from the U.S. Public Health Service made a new study. He agreed with the first team: muscle parasites carried by ticks.

1904: The next Public Health doctor totally disagreed. He wrote a long report, backed up by two hundred hours of staring into a microscope. His conclusion: No parasites, innocent ticks, and an 87 percent death rate. Rocky Mountain spotted fever was still a serious, deadly mystery.

1905: An Idaho doctor tried a secret experiment. He removed a bloated tick from a patient dying of the fever and put it on the arm of a prisoner in the local jail. Two days later, he moved the same tick to the leg of a woman volunteer. The prisoner came down with a severe case of the disease, but managed to survive. The woman had only mild symptoms.

For years, the doctor hid his illegal results. He had solved part of the mystery, but he didn't dare say so.

1906: Dr. Howard Taylor Ricketts arrived in Missoula, Montana, just inside the deadly valley. Some accounts say he came to Montana on vacation and stayed to help with the crisis, but if he did, he traveled with unusual baggage. Dr. Ricketts came with trunks full of the latest in scientific equipment, which he carefully set up in a sagging canvas tent he pitched himself on the hospital lawn. He also brought a good microscope and dozens of empty notebooks. Howard Ricketts had come to solve the mystery of Rocky Mountain spotted fever.

Howard grew up on a farm in Ohio, hunting and riding and tending cattle for his family and neighbors—all skills he would need later to solve his Montana mystery. Howard's parents, unlike their neighbors who thought grade school was more than enough, believed in college for their seven children.

Howard finished college, medical school, and a residency in pathology (the study of disease and its causes), with a year in Berlin and another at the Pasteur Institute in Paris learning scientific skills. Meanwhile, he married Myra Tubbs, who waited twelve years for him to finish school.

Everyone who worked with Howard Ricketts agreed he was brilliant. He would need that, too, to solve the mystery.

Howard examined patients inside the Great Northern hospital. All had high fevers, severe head and muscle aches, and ugly spots covering most of their body. The spots started as small red dots on the wrists and ankles and slowly spread to large purplish-black blotches all over, including the soles of the feet. Somewhere between their sixth and twelfth day of illness, most patients died.

Cold baths, for fever, were the only real treatment. Quinine didn't work. Neither did creosote, arsenic, or any other drug doctors had tried.

Howard plunged right into the search for clues. He drew blood from the dying patients inside the hospital and took it outside to his tent.

First, he removed the fiber from diseased human blood (so the blood, itself, wouldn't harm the animals) and injected it into several rabbits. Not much luck. Next, he tried guinea pigs.

Instant success. The first two guinea pigs came down with symptoms matching the ones human patients had. One died. He tried a second pair, injecting blood from the first animals. One became sick. "Astonishing," Howard called it.

Howard knew he had actually transferred the infection—blood definitely carried the disease—but it seemed to weaken with each passage. Fresh animals injected with blood from the second pair showed no effects at all.

Next, Howard tried a monkey. Human victims' blood gave it a typical case of spotted fever.

Keeping careful notes on all his results, Howard filtered some contaminated blood through a special porcelain dish with tiny holes, designed to keep back blood cells and bacteria. He injected the straw-colored blood serum into new test guinea pigs. Nothing happened. Filtered blood had no effect.

That fact told Howard he was not hunting a virus. Viruses are small enough to pass through filters. Bacteria are held back by the right filter but are large enough to see through a microscope. Howard looked. He didn't see any. Other researchers had already tried. They had not seen any bacteria, either. So, what could be causing the mysterious disease?

Howard infected a second monkey. It died.

The mystery, as Howard Ricketts saw it, had two parts. First, what actually caused spotted fever? A tiny organism? A large virus? Poison? Something in the blood passed it on, but what? So far, he had no idea.

Second, how did spotted fever move? Doctors all agreed that it never spread from patient to patient. Something carried the disease directly to each victim. But what?

Howard decided to shift over to the second part of the mystery. He suspected he already knew the answer, judging from all the clues other researchers had uncovered.

Howard placed a small female tick just below the ear on one of his sick guinea pigs and watched it burrow under the hair. Two days later, he carefully removed it and put it in a box, to let it get hungry again.

In another two days he let it bite just below the ear of a healthy animal. Four days later, the second guinea pig came down with the fever.

Howard knew how a scientific investigation should be done.

In each experiment, he set up controls, to make sure he was really testing what he thought he was testing.

As he injected contaminated human blood into some animals, he injected healthy human blood into others. At the same time he attached an infected tick to one guinea pig, he attached an uninfected tick (carefully grown by Howard, himself), to a different one. Each time, the controls stayed healthy.

To check for other factors, he put several control animals into the uncleaned cages where test guinea pigs had died of spotted fever. Not one became sick.

Then he had to stop the experiment. Howard had run out of guinea pigs.

While he waited for more animals to arrive, Howard dissected the bodies of the ones that had died. Almost every internal organ was affected, including the brain.

He also carried through on some experiments with ticks. By late summer, Howard could explain a wood tick's whole life cycle, and he knew that infected adult ticks of either sex could carry Rocky Mountain spotted fever. Since adult ticks only live for a few months in springtime, before laying their eggs and dying, Howard could explain the springtime "evil spirits."

Howard discovered that a tick needs at least two hosts. First the tiny tick larva latches onto some small animal, such as a squirrel or a mouse, to feed.

He made several camping trips into the canyons of Bitter Root Valley, just to observe. Howard found what he was looking for. Thousands and thousands of gophers, just waiting to be "lunch" for hungry baby ticks. He could understand why the Indians had thought the evil spirits inhabited gophers.

After a few days, the larva drop off to molt into nymphs.

They find another gopher, feed, then drop off again. Now, grown into adult ticks, they cling to tall grass, waiting for a large animal to pass. Elk and bear carry ticks, Howard found, but so do cows, horses, and humans. A trip by horseback through valley farms showed almost every farm animal covered with feeding ticks.

Back in his tent laboratory, using new guinea pigs, Howard transferred the fever back and forth from rodent to monkey. He discovered that bits of tissue from body organs could transfer disease as well as blood. Howard began to think some kind of poison spread through a victim's body. What else could it be?

As summer ended, Howard took down his tent and headed back to his main job at the University of Chicago. He took infected blood with him to study over the winter.

1907: Spring came, and a new epidemic arrived. So did Howard Ricketts. Mainly, the second year Howard studied ticks. Female ticks could pass the disease along in their eggs, he discovered, and the deadly disease could spread all through the ticks' bodies. Somehow, it didn't harm the eight-legged pests at all.

Dr. Ricketts could now offer some useful advice to the Montana Board of Health and to the frightened settlers. He had a plan. First, humans should try to avoid ticks. Second, horses and cows should be rubbed with oil, to keep ticks from attaching. Third, the gopher population should be poisoned.

Howard made a special trip back to Montana that winter, to try and interest the government in his plan. Almost no one listened. Howard went back to work on the first part of the mystery.

1908: Howard developed a vaccine, made from dried tick

eggs, which could ward off the disease if a victim received it within three days of a tick bite. Unfortunately, he couldn't make enough to vaccinate every tick-bitten person in Idaho and Montana, even if most people had wanted to give the vaccine a try. Mostly, people did not.

He pressed harder for the state to adopt his three-part plan. They stalled.

1909: Finally, after years of trying, Howard spotted something under the microscope. Using a new cell-staining technique, he could just make out some extremely tiny rod-shaped microorganisms in infected blood. Human, guinea pig, and monkey blood all showed the same mysterious cell-invading substance.

So did tick tissue and tick eggs. At least, Howard hoped he was seeing the same thing in all those places. The thing he was looking for seemed to be multiplying right inside the cells of its victims, like a super-tiny parasite. That, Howard knew, is what viruses do.

But he had already proved it wasn't a virus—at least, not any ordinary virus. It had to be many times larger than a normal virus, maybe half as large as an ordinary bacteria. Every time he tried to grow it, the mysterious substance disappeared.

Howard recorded all his findings in a fresh notebook. In his own mind, he had solved the mystery. Spotted fever was caused by a new kind of organism, somewhere between viruses and bacteria in size. As soon as he found a way to grow the organism in his lab, he would be ready to announce his discovery.

Meanwhile, the Montana legislature realized Dr. Ricketts was making valuable progress. They voted $6,000 for his use, in two more years of work. Unfortunately, the State Board of Examiners didn't agree. They considered research to be wasted money. Besides, the state treasury had already spent the money on a smallpox epidemic and no longer *had* $6,000. They wrote Howard not to come back.

Howard didn't want to quit, but he couldn't afford to finance all his own research. On Howard's desk was an offer from the government of Mexico to come and study the outbreak of typhus in Mexico City.

Typhus had symptoms in common with Rocky Mountain spotted fever. Maybe they were two forms of the same thing. Maybe he could take this new job and learn more about spotted fever at the same time. Howard wrote the Mexican officials to say that he would come.

In December, the Montana Board of Examiners reconsidered. They invited Howard back. They were too late.

That same month, Howard and his portable lab took the train to Mexico. He got right to work. Howard quickly figured out that typhus, while almost as deadly as spotted fever, is not the same disease. But it did seem to be caused by a similar super-tiny organism. Howard spent hours glued to his microscope.

He knew his test samples could be deadly. He handled them with care.

One spring day, while transferring infected lice from one part of his laboratory to another, Howard let his caution slip. A week later, he died of typhus fever.

Later researchers realized that Howard had already solved the mystery. He had discovered a completely unsuspected new form of microorganism, related to both viruses and bacteria, which could cause dozens of diseases in humans and animals.

All of them seem to be spread by tiny carriers such as lice and ticks. Biologists named an entire order of similar organisms after him. The particular "something" he had spent so many years hunting is called *Rickettsia rickettsi*, in his memory.

Within a few years, farmers and ranchers were using Howard Ricketts' plan to cut down on the number of ticks. While stamping them out completely is impossible, the number of disease-carrying ticks in Montana and Idaho has been cut to a tiny fraction of what it was in 1906. Rocky Mountain spotted fever, thanks to Howard Ricketts and others, is now rare.

# 5

# THE CASE OF THE ASTOUNDING REBOUND

McGill University, Montreal, Canada, 1903: Ernest Rutherford stared at the smudged, slightly foggy photographic plate and wondered if he should throw it away. Maybe the plate was defective. He developed another and found the same puzzling blur, right where a sharp, thin line ought to be. What was going wrong?

Ernest Rutherford, a young physicist from New Zealand, had just photographed a clue to the greatest mystery facing scientists at the turn of the century, but he didn't realize it. The trouble was, the mystery was too small to see.

The clue in the fuzzy photo came from inside an atom. What was an atom like, inside? Nobody knew. For centuries, no one even cared.

Democritus, the ancient Greek philosopher, thought the world was made from atoms, but he didn't see anything mysterious about them. Atoms, he stated around 400 B.C., are the smallest bits matter can be divided into. Nothing can be smaller. In fact, "atom," in Greek, means "indivisible."

The nineteenth-century scientists didn't see any problem, either. They studied the behavior of atoms, but not the insides. No one suspected an atom even *had* insides.

Then, in 1897, J.J. Thomson uncovered the mystery. Sir Joseph John Thomson, British physicist, headed Cambridge University's famous Cavendish Laboratory. Everyone called him J.J.

J.J. never planned to look inside an atom. He intended to study electricity, using a special instrument called a *cathode ray tube*.

Cathode ray tubes are used today to make the images on television and computer screens. In J.J.'s day, the device was a way to see moving electricity.

J.J.'s confusing discovery involved a clear glass "bottle," with openings at both ends, into which scientists inserted tiny metal plates. To make it work, they pumped out most of the air and forced electric current in at one end—called the "cathode." An eerie, green-glowing beam traveled straight across the vacuum to the other, or "anode" end. They named the glowing beam a "cathode ray."

But what *were* cathode rays? Were they some kind of wave energy, like ripples in a stream, or were they particles, like a spray of machine-gun bullets?

J.J. and his assistants tried a test. Could an electrical field make the speedy rays change their path? Students aimed the rays through a slit in the anode and into another vacuum tube containing two small metal plates. When they connected live batteries, one plate became charged with positive electricity and one charged with negative.

Nothing happened to the glowing rays. They sped straight ahead. Electricity should not affect waves, so some scientists considered the question solved. The rays had to be waves.

J.J. disagreed. He guessed that cathode rays must be some kind of super-tiny particle, but he needed evidence. He puzzled over the problem for weeks, thinking about it even when he was out on the golf course. Then he thought of a way to prove his theory.

The particles he pictured in his mind had to be so small that atoms in the air would be like giant suns surrounding them. Maybe the gas left in a cathode ray tube was interfering. Maybe the vacuum wasn't good enough.

Vacuum pumps had been giving scientists trouble for years. None of them could get all the air out of a glass tube. But a new model of pump had just been delivered to Cavendish. J.J. decided to try the whole experiment again.

Using the new equipment, J.J. and his students pumped a cathode ray tube emptier than ever before. Then they turned on the electrical field.

This time, in front of everybody, the beam curved gently toward the positive plate. Everyone could see the shining spot of light at the end of the tube. Only a stream of negatively charged particles would act exactly that way.

J.J. Thomson's Nobel Prize-winning effort proved his favorite theory—that cathode rays are actually tiny particles of negative electricity. He named them "corpuscles" (later renamed "electrons"). In further experiments, he found that they were more than 10,000 times tinier than the smallest atoms in size, and that they weighed almost 2,000 times less.

Now, the next mystery began. What were they, and where did they come from?

Using the new pump, graduate students at Cavendish retried all their old experiments. No matter what gas or metal or salt they placed at the cathode, no matter what gas they left in the tube, exactly the same "corpuscles" came streaming out.

The answer, said J.J., was obvious. "Corpuscles" are part of an atom—in fact, a built-in part of every atom.

That explanation startled other scientists, at Cavendish and worldwide. Everything they had ever learned told them atoms never broke into parts.

"I was brought up to look at the atom as a nice hard fellow, red or gray in colour, according to taste," said Ernest Rutherford, one of J.J.'s favorite students and occasional golfing partner.

But other hints that atoms might not be simply "nice hard fellows" had been piling up for years. Clues came in at different times and places, but it was J.J. Thomson who added them all together. His students, at a banquet, summed it up in a poem:

All preconceived notions he set at defiance
By means of some neat and ingenious appliance
By which he discovers some new law of science
which no-one had ever suspected before.
All the chemists went off into fits;
Some of them thought they were losing their wits,
when quite without warning
(Their theories scorning)
The atom one morning
He broke into bits.

(from Alex Keller's *The Infancy of Atomic Physics*)

Obviously the ancient Greeks—and almost every scientist since—had been wrong. Atoms were not indivisible at all. Atoms were like tiny "locked rooms," with something complex going on inside. Atoms held a hidden mystery.

J.J. thought the solution to this new mystery was also obvious. He pictured a fuzzy sphere of positive electricity, with "his" negative electrons embedded inside. He compared the atom to a "plum pudding" (raisin bread is a good, modern substitute), where the "pudding" stood for the positive mass of the atom; electrons were the "plums."

Not everyone was sure the famous J.J. had it right, this time. In 1903, Philipp Lenard, a German physicist, described the atom as mostly empty space, with tiny electrons and positive particles floating around in pairs. The next year a Japanese physicist, Hantaro Nagaoka, proposed that electrons might be moving around a central nucleus, something like the "rings move around the planet Saturn."

None of the three theories could be seriously tested. No one knew how. The mystery had to be abandoned, temporarily.

Meanwhile, Ernest Rutherford, former Cavendish student, had other problems on his mind. Radioactivity, not atoms, was Rutherfords's main love. He supposed that J.J. was probably right about his "plum pudding" atom, but he didn't give the mystery much thought.

Rutherford, now a respected scientist, had moved to Canada, to head the physics laboratory at McGill University. Rutherford had started his career with a different kind of mystery. How could a shy farm boy, fourth of twelve children in a poor family, manage to get anywhere?

No one in Spring Grove, New Zealand, suspected "Ern,"

born in 1871, was brilliant, but they noticed one thing about him. When he studied, he really studied. Schoolmates joked that you could "hit him on the head with a stick" while he was reading, and he wouldn't notice.

Ernest used that same concentration all his life. In school he won scholarship after scholarship, building a record of excellence in everything from football to physics.

Then good luck changed his life. Ernest placed second in the competition for a scholarship to Cambridge University, in England.

The first-place winner turned down the prize. He wanted to get married. Ernest wanted to get married, too, but he told his girl friend, Mary Newton, their plans would have to wait. (Five years later he came back for her.)

The story goes that he was digging potatoes when his mother came running out with the news about the scholarship. He threw down the shovel and announced, "That's the last potato I shall ever dig."

Now, at McGill, Rutherford had "a swell lab under my control," as he wrote Mary. He had already sorted out and named two kinds of radioactivity—alpha and beta. Now he recognized a third, gamma rays.

Radiation "still remains a mystery," he wrote. If radiation comes out of atoms, what are atoms like, inside? How could anyone find out?

Ernest's next project uncovered an unexpected clue. With the help of chemist Frederick Soddy, he discovered that radioactive atoms actually transmute, or change themselves into other kinds of atoms, as they give off radiation. In fact, most of them, given enough time (which may be millions of years), eventually change themselves into lead.

This discovery was so startling it was hard even for Soddy and Rutherford to believe. "For Mike's sake, Soddy, don't call it transmutation," Rutherford warned. "They'll have our heads off as alchemists." It didn't take long to realize no other word would do.

Actually, it was a kind of "reverse alchemy," reporters of the day told their readers. Instead of scientists trying to transform lead into rare metals, rare metals were changing themselves into lead.

The discovery caused total confusion among scientists and the public. Atoms turning into different atoms? All by themselves? It didn't make sense, but it made Rutherford famous.

Rutherford ignored the uproar. He like to keep things simple.

Most days, Rutherford kept to the same routines, giving lectures (frequently far over his students' heads) and sitting on a wooden lab stool to watch and talk with "the boys" at work. When he was feeling most content, he strolled through the lab singing "Onward, Christian Soldiers," slightly off-key.

Mainly, he worked on his own research. And soon, another clue to the atomic puzzle surfaced. Rutherford had been trying to measure the speed of alpha particles, letting a thin stream of them pass through a series of slits in a matchbox-sized metal box. He had developed a large stack of photographic plates, each with one narrow, definite band of light marking where the alpha particles landed.

Then Rutherford slipped a slice of mica between the alpha source and the photographic film. Mica is a rocky crystal which can be split into transparent sheets, thinner than paper.

Mica didn't affect the particles' speed at all, but when

Rutherford developed his first photograph, he noticed that the clear line of light had turned blurry. The alpha particles no longer all landed on the same spot.

The fuzzy image totally confused Rutherford. He had expected alpha particles to pass through mica "like cannonballs in a hailstorm."

Rutherford had built most of his equipment himself. Now, he took it all apart. Every piece passed a thorough inspection. Something, he decided, must be "scattering" the particles from their path as they sped through layers of mica atoms.

He did some calculations. According to his figures, an electrical field of 100 million volts per centimeter would be needed to shift particles as much as a few of them were shifting.

Ridiculous! How could an atom have such a gigantic electrical "punch"? The calculations didn't make sense. Rutherford put them away and went back to making measurements of alpha particles.

Then two major upheavals shelved Rutherford's experiments for a while. In 1907 he became Director of the physics laboratory at Manchester, England. The next year he won a Nobel Prize.

The Nobel Prize surprised Rutherford most. Since it honored his discovery of transmutation, or atoms changing from one kind into another, the Swedish Royal Academy awarded the prize in Chemistry. Rutherford joked, in his acceptance speech, that "the quickest transformation" was himself "from a physicist into a chemist."

Money from the Nobel Prize—close to 7,000 pounds, when a year's salary was 1,600 pounds—came in handy for the Rutherfords' new house with central heating. Manchester,

Rutherford wrote his mother in New Zealand, "felt colder" than Canada.

Rutherford set out to make the Manchester laboratory as fine as any lab anywhere. Some of the new equipment he built himself. It was quicker—and cheaper—than ordering from a catalog.

Rutherford discovered that the Chemistry Department had taken over several rooms assigned to physics. "By thunder," he protested at a faculty meeting, pounding his fist on the table. His red face got redder and his walrus-moustache quivered.

Everyone stared at this energetic new Director of Physics, still under forty, and looking "more like a farmer than a scientist." The chemists quickly moved out, replaced by physicists-in-training, who came from all over Europe and as far as Japan.

Finally, Rutherford turned his energy back to research. His new assistant, Hans Geiger, showed him a special kind of screen which flashed a microscopic spark of light every time an electrical impulse hit it. Zinc sulfide, on the screen, is phosphorescent. Electric charge makes it glow in the dark.

Alpha particles have an electric charge, so the flashing screen gave Rutherford a new way to study his "pet" project. He and Geiger placed a tiny sample of radium at one end of a metal vacuum tube fifteen feet long. A slow-but-steady stream of alpha particles traveled through the tube and hit the screen, while the rest were held back by the air or the radium's wrapping.

"It was possible," said an assistant, "to sit in a comfortable chair and see a spot of light on a screen move a few inches every time an alpha particle entered." For the first time in history, scientists could count separate atomic particles, not just try to measure a stream.

Rutherford's favorite lab, on the top floor under the roof, was much too light and airy for these experiments. Someone located an unused space in the basement, next to the photographic darkroom. The switch was no problem for the lab's Director. "I could do research at the North Pole," Rutherford used to boom.

Within days, students had turned the gloomy cellar into a working lab, filled with sturdy tables to hold their delicate instruments. To every newcomer, Rutherford or one of the others would point out a head-high hot water pipe to duck and two more water pipes to step over. Crickets chirped loudly in the daytime dark.

"Papa," as the graduate students called Rutherford, didn't have the patience to sit for long in the basement's feeble light, watching spots. Geiger (who would later invent the famous Geiger radiation counter) supervised most of that.

Geiger set up a tiny zinc sulfide screen. The glow-in-the dark material gave off a microscopic flash of light with each alpha particle hitting it.

Then the basement researchers placed a speck of radium behind a thin slit in a radiation shield. The particles passing through all landed on the screen in a fine, sharp line.

Individual flashes, called scintillations, were so small students needed a magnifying glass to see them clearly. (The whole apparatus had to be enclosed in a vacuum, so that air wouldn't spoil the results.) It was impossible to see individual scintillations, even with a magnifying glass, because they all fell on top of each other.

Rutherford suggested they try putting a barrier between the alpha source and the screen. When the students inserted a thin sheet of gold foil, the line immediately blurred. The particles seemed to spread out, or "scatter" across the screen, instead of falling neatly on a line.

Now, the watchers could see individual scintillations. When they removed the foil, the sharp line of light reappeared on the screen.

As Rutherford had noticed years before, sliding mica or some other super-thin barrier between a source of alpha particles and a photographic plate caused the light image on the plate to blur. No one knew why, and no one had ever tried to investigate. Now, in 1908, the scientists could actually see the light blur, not just take its picture.

The fuzzy blur widened with heavier sheets of gold or platinum or aluminum foil and narrowed when the sheets were thinner, usually around one fifty-thousandth of an inch thick. Even so, most particles only "scattered" by small angles.

If they used anything thicker than a delicate foil—even a heavy piece of paper—as a barrier, the glow stopped entirely. Alpha particles cannot penetrate barriers more than a few micrometers thick.

The mystery had resurfaced, from a new direction. J.J. Thompson had discovered tiny particles inside every atom. What else lay hidden in there? The flashing screen began to uncover a new, major clue.

Scattering took over the conversation for days at the tea-and-cookies meetings Rutherford held every afternoon. Most people guessed that something in the metal was causing the particles to bounce, like a football hitting a rock.

Only a few particles took big bounces, well off to the side. Probably the larger deviations were just an accumulation of small scatterings, all happening in the same direction.

Were any particles scattering all the way off the screen, Rutherford wondered? The possibility was on his mind when Hans Geiger came to him with a question about a new student.

"Don't you think Marsden ought to begin a small research?" Geiger asked. Ernest Marsden had been working at Manchester for a short time, but he hadn't yet earned his degree.

Rutherford didn't have to think long. "Why not let him see if any alpha particles can be scattered through a large angle?"

Rutherford did not believe any would be. He was sure alpha particles were too energetic and fast. The easy and probably boring project ought to be just the thing to keep an undergraduate assistant busy for a week or so.

Two or three days later, Geiger came rushing into Rutherford's office, obviously excited. "We have been able to get some of the alpha particles coming backwards!" he said.

Rutherford looked up, stunned. "It was," he said later, "quite the most incredible event that has ever happened to me in my life. It was almost as incredible as if you fired a fifteen-inch shell at a piece of tissue paper and it came back and hit you." It was the biggest clue yet, to the mystery.

What kind of force could exist inside a tissue-thin sheet of gold foil with the power to stop a particle moving at 10,000 miles per second and send it flying backwards? No one even had a guess. No one could unravel the new clue.

Marsden and Geiger redid the experiment a new way, while Rutherford sat on a stool to watch. They carefully arranged a shielded, glass-enclosed radium source at an angle to the foil barrier. The foil now became a reflector, working like a mirror which lets you see around a corner. Rebounding alphas bounced past the lead shield onto the screen itself.

Albert Einstein said, later, the technique was "like shooting sparrows in the dark," but it worked each and every time. A few alpha particles always hit the foil and flew backwards.

Marsden sat for hours, counting every flash with a low-power microscope. The crew logged more than 100,000 scintillations.

Thicker foil caused more rebounds, but only up to a certain point. Then the level stayed the same, no matter how thick the barrier. Again, no one could explain why.

Rutherford and his crew uncovered one final, surprising fact. Different metals scattered different amounts. About one particle in 8,000 flew backwards from platinum foil. Gold rebounded fifty times more particles than aluminum did. No one could explain how.

Rutherford spent more than a year mulling over the totally unexpected facts and trying to mesh them with everything else he knew about atoms. He must have had a pretty clear idea right away, but in science, ideas come easy. The proof and the complete explanation matter most.

Rutherford did some of his best thinking when he could get away from the commotion of the busy laboratory. Often he went back to the lab late at night, looking for quiet. Sometimes he and Geiger drove out in the "fresh air" in his new fourteen-mile-per-hour Wolseley-Siddeley automobile. (The car's speed could push up to thirty-five, but Rutherford had to be wary of "high speeds," because of "motor traps" along the road, and "a ten-guinea fine if I am caught.")

Finally, just before Christmas, 1910, the clucs began to pull together. Rutherford walked into Geiger's office "in the best of spirits." He had solved the rest of the mystery in his head. He now knew what the atom looked like. He could, Rutherford told his friend, "explain everything."

As usual, he had worked out all the details in his precise mathematics. Only one thing, he explained, could possibly stop and reverse a small, fast, charged object. That had to be a bigger object with a much bigger charge.

That "bigger" object had to be extremely small, itself, some 10,000 times smaller than the size of the atom. It could only be a "heavy center" (later named the nucleus), containing all the positive charge and almost all of the mass of the atom, collected in one tiny spot.

Since atoms are electrically neutral, their negative charge had to be spread thinly around the positive center. In other words, electrons circled around this nucleus, somewhat (but not exactly) like tiny planets around the sun. This idea, and no other, fit all the facts. J.J.'s "plum pudding" atom was all wrong.

Now that he knew the answer, calculations which had seemed ridiculous back in 1903 made perfect sense. In fact, the facts all fit so well that Rutherford's new theory could even predict just how many particles would be scattered and by how much.

Rutherford and Geiger set up experiments that same day to test the predictions. This time, Rutherford sat patiently in the dark, watching for sparks of light. Every detail of the new theory checked out perfectly.

Rutherford announced his momentous discovery at a dinner party of scientists the next Sunday, in the spring of 1911.

Rutherford's discovery, said one famous scientist, started the greatest change in our ideas about matter since the time of

Democritus, twenty-three centuries ago. All the modern advances in nuclear physics are built on it.

Years later another scientist, talking about atomic discoveries, told Rutherford he had been "lucky to be riding the crest of a wave."

"Lucky, nothing," Rutherford is said to have responded. "I *made* the wave."

# 6

# THE CURIOUS QUANTUM MYSTERY

A sudden crime wave stalks the city. Witnesses each describe a different figure, maybe male or female, white or black, young or old. Detectives flounder on each case, until they realize they are all chasing the same suspect—a master of disguises.

Classical physicists thought they had learned everything. They were already advising their brightest students to take up some other field. Physics, they said, was finished. Only a few "loose ends" needed wrapping up.

Then a wave of mysteries took physics by surprise. The facts seemed to wear a different disguise for each investigator. Clues turned up in unusual places, all pointing to the same elusive, unlikely suspect.

Case #1, Berlin, Germany, 1900: Max Planck thought he must be crazy. So did everyone else. When Max Karl Ernst Ludwig Planck, German physicist, began to study "black-bodies" he meant to tie up a "loose end" of classical physics, not uncover a major mystery.

A many-talented man, Planck picked physics over music as a career, calling it "the most sublime scientific pursuit in life." He was no rebel. Herr Professor Planck believed in old-fashioned physics, and he enjoyed working with its laws almost as much as he enjoyed his yearly mountain-climbing vacations.

Scientists already knew that heated objects give off, or radiate, energy waves, in much the same way that a pond ripples when you toss in a rock. They had developed some theories about the *frequency* of those waves, which means the number of waves passing per second.

But what physicists found, when they began actually measuring the frequency of heat waves, was a mystery. The evidence didn't fit their theories.

Classical physics said frequency ought to be totally random—with any frequency as likely as any other. But according to experiments, it wasn't. Even more unexpected, researchers kept finding the same, specific frequencies again and again, instead of the wide variation they expected to measure.

Max Planck doubted the evidence, not the theories. Why, Planck wondered, couldn't an object radiate with whatever frequency it wanted?

Could classical physics be wrong? Planck didn't think so. Some key had to be missing. He decided to find it.

A theoretical physicist, forty-two-year-old Planck did not spend long hours in a laboratory. He worked with ideas, and he could think wherever he pleased. Every day he took long walks in the countryside, working problems in his head. And every night, to clear the same problems out of his mind, Planck played complex and beautiful music on the piano.

To solve the frequency question, Max Planck pictured a

"blackbody." In physics, a blackbody is the name for a completely imaginary object which can—in theory—absorb or give off any frequency of radiation. He worked out calculations for every possible frequency, struggling for months over figures which told him what he didn't want to hear.

Finally, he had to admit the truth. If all frequencies were possible, then his imaginary "blackbody" would be giving off energy from all of them, all of the time. In other words, an infinite amount of energy—all the energy of the world—would be coming out of one small object! That was obvious nonsense. Something had to be seriously wrong, and Planck knew it wasn't his calculations.

He took a closer look at the laboratory situation. In the lab, only specific wave frequencies seemed to be possible. Any others, falling in-between, were somehow "forbidden."

Planck had hoped to prove the experimenters wrong. Instead, he seemed to be proving them right. His figures kept showing the same thing: only certain frequencies are possible.

Classical physics couldn't explain the mystery. Planck needed new clues. Unfortunately for his pride, he knew just where to look.

A colleague in Austria, Ludwig Boltzmann, had recently published some theories suggesting that nothing was really certain, and that unlikely events, such as a rock lifting from the ground by itself, might actually be possible (even though highly improbable). Probability, he said, governed everything. Boltzmann used statistics to calculate the probability of each law of physics holding true.

Planck had called Boltzmann's work total nonsense. Now, against his better judgment, Planck began to use some probability statistics in his own calculations. He began treating energy as a "bunch of tiny things," not a series of waves. "After a few weeks of the most strenuous work in my life," Planck said later, "the darkness lifted."

The only workable answer—though Planck didn't quite believe it, himself—was that energy moved in sudden jumps or spurts, like super-tiny packets of power. "Discontinuously," Planck called it. He named the packets "quanta," from the Latin word for "how much."

A "blackbody," or any other object, could radiate energy in amounts of one or ten or millions of quanta, but never one-half. Quanta came in different sizes, but not in fractions. The idea is something like ordering Small, Medium, or Large soft drinks at a fast-food chain. Millions of each size are sold daily, but not even one falls in-between.

Using quanta, Planck experimented with a formula for calculating energy from frequency or frequency from energy. To his great surprise, the formula worked.

To his greater surprise, his formula provided a new number—a universal constant relating frequency to energy. The lowest amount of energy possible at any frequency, divided by that frequency, always gave the same numerical answer—always, for any frequency of light or heat. Planck labeled the new constant *h*. In modern terms, *h* calculates to be $6.626176 \times 10^{-34}$ (or 0.000000000000000000000000000000000626176) joule-second, in units of energy multiplied by time.

With *h*, Planck could calculate energies for light coming from hot metals and even from distant stars. Everywhere he tested it, the formula,

$$E = h\nu$$

where E is energy and $\nu$ (a Greek letter, pronounced "nu") is frequency, gave the right answer.

Planck's constant is too small to worry about, when physics deals with moving people or machines. That's why no one had ever noticed it before. The "key" Planck had found, instead of proving classical physics right, had opened a whole unsuspected world of super-small physics.

Planck didn't much like his new quantum idea. In fact, he hated it. Light in tiny packets? Max Planck, like other physicists, had always been sure energy moved in a continuous stream.

To make matters worse, he hadn't even done the math quite right. Planck had forgotten one final step, where Boltzmann always summed up, or "reintegrated" his statistical results.

Planck suspected the whole thing was just a mathematical "trick," which somehow happened to work. He shared his quantum theory with other scientists cautiously. Some of them thought he had lost his mind. Only one person knew Planck had seen through the first "disguise" in an ongoing mystery.

Case #2, Bern, Switzerland, 1905: Albert Einstein, German physicist, saw Planck's work as a valuable clue. To test it, he chose another classical mystery called the *photoelectric effect.* When strong light bounces off a piece of metal, it immediately knocks out a few electrons. The energy of the electrons knocked out depends only upon the frequency of the light beam used. No one knew what happened or why.

Einstein, twenty-six, studied Planck's strange new quantum theory, and he did some thinking. Einstein didn't trust the packet idea, but if it worked for light waves radiating out of some object, why not for light rays hitting some other object?

What if Planck's quanta acted like little billiard balls, crashing into electrons and knocking them around? The more energetic the quanta, the more energetic the electron they could dislodge.

Einstein worked in a patent office that year, not in a physics laboratory. He had never done well in school, he didn't yet have a Ph.D., and physics was more a hobby than a profession. Still, thinking, his greatest talent, didn't need a lab or a degree. Einstein had read about other people's experiments. Low-frequency red light always knocked out low-energy electrons and high-frequency violet light knocked out high.

He tried some calculations, built on Planck's constant. They worked. Then he noticed something that "at first," Einstein said, "had been hidden." Planck had handled the math wrong.

It was "most fortunate for the development of physics," Einstein said later, that he didn't see Planck's errors right away. If he had, he would never have bothered with quanta at all.

Einstein began to look deeper. At first, he only found more mathematical errors. Planck had not thought the whole matter through clearly enough. "If Planck had," Einstein said, "he probably would not have made his great discovery."

The idea was too useful to throw away. It worked, even though it should not have. The answers always came out right.

After some background checking, Einstein took a bold step. He decided to use Planck's formula, anyway. Einstein labeled the decision a "heuristic principle." Heuristic means something that helps solve a problem but is, itself, questionable or unprovable. The perfect word to fit the situation!

Then Albert Einstein, who would later become the world's most famous physicist, carried Planck's idea one step further. He predicted energy not only came in quanta, energy *was* quanta. In other words, instead of waves, Einstein's idea said that energy had to be made of tiny particles. More intense light simply meant more particles, but a different frequency of light meant a different "size" of quanta, or light-particle. His calculations fit all the experimental evidence perfectly, explaining why ultraviolet light causes sunburn when visible light doesn't and even why X-rays kill bacteria. Higher frequencies mean more powerful quanta.

Unfortunately, that confused everybody. If classical physicists all agreed on one thing, it was that light always traveled in waves, not particles. Many scientists made fun of Einstein's paper.

Planck, himself, thought Einstein had pushed the quantum idea too far. Another physicist wrote that Einstein's work, "appears in every case to predict exactly the observed results," but that the idea behind the work was "bold, not to say reckless." Einstein had unmasked disguise #2, but the overall picture only seemed more mysterious.

Case #3, England, 1913: When Niels Henrik David Bohr stepped off the ship from Denmark in the fall of 1911 and took a train to Cavendish Laboratory, he had an entirely different mystery on his mind: the inside of an atom. What was it like?

Bohr, who liked to comb his blond hair straight back from his forehead, got into trouble the very first week at Cavendish. "This is incorrect," he blurted to J.J. Thomson, the lab's famous director. Bohr's English was so poor he couldn't even explain that he meant Thomson's "plum pudding" model of the atom, or that he had been looking forward for months to talking atoms with J.J. The director was not impressed.

Bohr's relationship with J.J. never quite recovered, but his fluency in English quickly improved. It had to. The lanky Danish physicist was a thinker, not an experimenter, and he did his best thinking out loud.

Shy socially, Bohr was always outspoken when the conversation involved physics. Arguing physics was his main hobby. (Niels also loved soccer, but felt inferior to his brother, who made the Danish Olympic team in 1908.)

Anyway, the argument with Thomson no longer mattered. "Plum pudding" was essentially dead. Ernest Rutherford had announced his theory about a nuclear atom, picturing a positive charge in the center and negative electrons moving around it.

Bohr met this new theory with a new argument, and he transferred his scholarship over to Manchester, so he could work—and argue—directly with Rutherford. Bohr loved Rutherford's model of the atom, except for one detail. It could not possibly work!

Bohr didn't worry about that. He never let details get in his way.

Eventually, an electron circling around a positive center would have to run out of energy. Everything classical physicists knew about motion pointed to that result. Rutherford agreed. He only intended his idea to be a rough picture. How the atom really worked was still a mystery.

Rutherford's picture of the atom needed "a radical change," said twenty-six-year-old Bohr, and he had a plan: ignore everything classical physics taught and try something new. He found a clue in Max Planck's not-quite-believable quantum theory. Bohr liked that theory much better than Planck did.

What, Bohr wondered, if electrons act just like light? What if they have only certain quanta of energy available? They could not gradually "wind down," as classical physics predicted. The idea is something like having only a dollar bill, with no change. It's impossible to spend a quarter, or even a penny.

Bohr pictured the electrons in an atom as having all their energy locked up in tidy little packets. They could circle the nucleus forever, until something disturbed them. Then they could give off (or take in) a quantum of energy. The energy change would cause them to shift immediately from one orbit to another. Bohr described this as a "quantum jump."

The idea of electrons "jumping" from one orbit to another was about as popular with classical physicists as if Bohr had tried to tell them Mars suddenly jumped into Earth's orbit. Bohr didn't worry. He was beginning to realize that the workings of an atom couldn't quite *be* pictured in ordinary terms.

Bohr took the idea further. Only certain orbits in an atom are possible, he predicted. Electrons can move from one to another, but—just as Planck had said about heat waves—never in-between. Nothing in the solar system illustrated that theory, either.

Bohr tinkered with the idea for months, with only one important interruption. He couldn't put off sailing back to Denmark to get married. It didn't take long, though, because Bohr convinced his new bride, Margrethe, to skip their honeymoon. He wanted to get right back to work.

Unfortunately, the atom mystery was far from solved. Energy in quanta brought up as many questions as it answered. The more Bohr tried to perfect his new model of the atom, the more it fell apart. He felt stumped. His scholarship year ended, and Bohr and Margrethe went back to Copenhagen.

Then a friend reminded Bohr of something he already knew. A glowing substance radiates energy in a specific pattern of frequencies as identifiable as a fingerprint. This pattern is called a spectrum. It shows up on film as a pattern of lines, looking something like the price codes on grocery items. Every element, whether alone or combined, has a spectrum, but no one could explain why.

Nor could anyone explain why an atom should have so many spectral lines. One physicist said hydrogen, the simplest atom, appeared to be "more complicated than a grand piano."

A Swiss high school teacher named Johann Balmer, in 1885 (the year Bohr was born), had written a formula relating the spectral lines of hydrogen to each other. Balmer didn't understand why spectra happened; he simply saw the mathematical relationship as an interesting curiosity. Bohr knew it had to be the clue he needed.

"As soon as I saw Balmer's formula," said Bohr, "the whole thing was immediately clear to me."

Balmer's formula showed that the spectral lines of hydrogen are related. Planck's formula, as Bohr applied it, could finally show *how* they are related. The distance from one line to another always turned out to include a small, whole number multiplied by $h$. One or two or three, but never one-half! Quanta at work!

Best of all, Bohr could now explain *why* spectral lines are related. The spectral lines of hydrogen show an electron jumping in or out of its possible orbits, as it absorbs or gives off energy.

Finally, Bohr's confusing, imaginary orbits had a basis in fact. So, at last, did Max Planck's constant, $h$. "A little piece of reality," Bohr called it.

Bohr patched together bits from classical and quantum physics in a long, complex paper explaining atomic structure. He sent it first to Rutherford, who agreed with the ideas but wanted to shorten the paper. That suggestion horrified Bohr so much he sailed all the way from Denmark back to England, just to argue with Rutherford about it.

Bohr held out. Rutherford corrected his errors in English, but didn't cut a word, and Bohr published not just one, but a series of lengthy papers describing his picture of the atom.

Bohr's papers dealt only with hydrogen, but other physicists quickly applied his work to more complex elements. Even more exciting, chemists used Bohr's orbits to explain how each kind of atom is related to every other. Any new theory with so many practical uses had to be correct. Some scientists called Bohr's work "ingenious," (although a few others, including J.J. Thomson, remained unconvinced).

Planck, Einstein, and Bohr, the three fathers of quantum theory, each received a Nobel Prize for his part in the solution: Planck in 1918, Einstein in 1921 (he actually got the prize for this discovery, and not for the more famous Theory of Relativity), and Bohr in 1922.

But Bohr's papers left other questions unanswered. His hodgepodge, pieced-together atom had uncovered "disguise" #3, but he hadn't solved the whole quantum mystery. That had to wait for a new generation of scientists.

# 7

# SWEET DEATH

The mysterious illness—a mass murderer of the deadliest kind—caused people to lose weight while eating huge quantities of food. Victims produced so much urine British doctors called it the "pissing disease." Eventually, the victims all died.

Patients suffering from diabetes mellitus had been dying for centuries, and no one knew why. In Roman times, doctors thought the body dissolved away in its own sugar-filled urine, which tasted (the test doctors used until about 200 years ago) as sweet as honey. Even a diabetic's blood tasted of sugar. No victim escaped, and no doctor knew what to do.

Clues to the mysterious illness began turning up. First, researchers discovered that removal of a soft, oblong-shaped body organ called the pancreas, located below and behind the stomach, always brought on the killer disease. Somehow the pancreas seemed to control diabetes. But how? No one had a guess.

The next clue almost slipped by. In 1869, a young German medical student named Paul Langerhans, looking through his microscope at a slice of pancreas, spotted some tiny "islands" of odd-looking tissue hidden inside. He had no idea what they could be.

That discovery led to a major clue. Every time doctors did an autopsy on someone who had died of diabetes, they found the mysterious little "islands" shrunken and dried up—even if the rest of the pancreas looked healthy. Could those strange "islets of Langerhans" have something to do with diabetes? No one knew how to find out.

Meanwhile, doctors tried prescribing a high-calorie diet. Patients, their urine full of sugar, slipped into comas and died. Next, doctors tried a diet high in fat but low in carbohydrates (especially sugar). Diabetics died just as quickly.

Researchers all over the world worked on the mystery. Slowly, they began to understand the clue they had all been ignoring: a diabetic patient's body simply cannot handle food. Any food. An "overdose" only makes the problem worse.

Doctors began to put their patients on starvation diets, allowing no carbohydrates—which seemed to cause the worst problems—and barely enough fat and protein to stay alive. The low-cal treatment worked, in a way. Victims began living longer.

Unfortunately, they lived with constant hunger, looked as thin as skeletons, and often felt too weak to stand up. By 1921, the mystery of diabetes was no closer to a solution.

That winter, Dr. Frederick Grant Banting had his own problems. A twenty-nine-year-old Canadian surgeon just back from World War I, Fred planned to specialize in orthopedic surgery. Day after day, Fred sat in his empty office waiting for patients to arrive. Almost no one did.

Living on borrowed money, engaged to a young woman he couldn't afford to marry, Fred helped support himself by giving lectures at a nearby medical school. One evening he prepared a lesson on carbohydrate metabolism—a subject he knew almost nothing about.

Fred searched through textbooks and magazines, looking for information on how the body digests and uses carbohydrates. Several of his sources mentioned diabetes, where metabolism breaks down.

That same night, reading in bed, Fred Banting happened on a new article on the mysterious disease in a just-arrived magazine. The article caught his attention. Maybe he could mention it in his lecture.

Instead, Fred discovered the mystery. The more he read, the more fascinated he became.

Researchers, the article said, believe some mysterious secretion must be coming from the tiny islets of Langerhans inside a normal pancreas, to help a body metabolize food. Since a normal pancreas also produces strong digestive juices, the pancreas had to be a double organ. It made two separate kinds of secretions.

But whenever scientists tried to collect the "hidden" secretion, the outer digestive juices somehow destroyed it—whatever it was. Injecting whole, ground-up pancreas into a diabetic animal didn't help. Nothing anyone had tried worked.

Fred kept reading. Then the magazine mentioned a new clue. It described what happened when an accidental obstruction shut off the blood supply to one patient's pancreas. The organ withered, but the tiny islets inside stayed healthy and functioning. Most important, *the patient did not get diabetes!*

Fred dropped off to sleep. About 2:00 A.M., he woke and sat up in bed. He had a fabulous idea.

Suppose, he thought, a surgeon operated on a dog and tied off the blood supply to its pancreas. The organ would wither. It would stop producing its normal digestive juices. Then, maybe, the surgeon could remove that dead pancreas and maybe—just maybe—the islets would still be working. Maybe the atrophied pancreas could be ground up and used to treat diabetes.

The idea sounded far more exciting than sitting in an empty office every day. Fred decided to tackle the diabetes mystery.

First, he needed a laboratory. The school where he lectured referred him to Dr. John James Rickard Macleod at the University of Toronto, where Fred had graduated from medical school. He outlined his idea to the frowning professor.

J.J.R. Macleod knew the idea Fred was so excited about had already been tried. It hadn't worked. In fact, he knew far more about the diabetes mystery than Fred did. He stared skeptically at the tall young surgeon sitting in his office.

Macleod thought Fred Banting had no hope of success. Still, a carefully done failure might uncover a fresh clue or two. A few weeks later he gave a cautious okay to the project and offered a small unused laboratory, borrowed equipment, some dogs left over from another project, and—since he knew Fred was not much of a chemist—an assistant. Charles Best, graduate student in biochemistry, drew the assistant's assignment.

Macleod did not offer payment. Fred would be as poor as ever.

The third floor room Dr. Macleod assigned them had tables, benches, sinks, and, according to Fred, the "dirt of the years" in it. He and Charley scrubbed the walls, the floor, and even the ceiling. By the middle of May, everything was ready.

Macleod helped Banting draw up a plan of action—first, operate on a dog and remove most of its pancreas, leaving a little flap tucked up under the skin. As long as some pancreas remained, the dog would not develop diabetes. Let it recover from surgery. Then remove the remaining piece of pancreas (a much simpler operation). Overnight, the dog would become diabetic.

Fred and Charley planned to do this with several dogs. They needed to get familiar with the symptoms of diabetes and the blood and urine tests needed to study them. These dogs would all die.

They chose several other dogs for a different operation. This time they would open the dog, tie a suture tightly around the blood supply to its pancreas, and close the incision. Weeks later, they would reoperate and find, hopefully, that the pancreas had degenerated. They could remove it and extract the mystery secretion. Or maybe they could graft a piece of the withered pancreas into a diabetic dog. They hadn't quite decided.

Fred had never removed a pancreas. He had never done serious surgery on a dog. Professor Macleod helped with the first case, a female brown spaniel. It seemed to go well.

Not so Fred Banting's first solo surgery. The dog died from an overdose of anesthetic. His second dog bled to death. Then the first dog, the spaniel, died from infection.

By the second week, the team had already killed all the "leftover" dogs, without a single success. Fred and Charley went out and bought more dogs from anyone willing to sell them.

Again and again they tried. By the middle of June, they had one diabetic dog, several recovering from first surgery, and seven dogs whose pancreatic ducts had been tied. Hopefully, their pancreases were degenerating, inside. No one knew for sure.

Then Professor Macleod wished them good luck and left for his summer vacation. Fred and Charley were on their own.

For the whole, hot summer of 1921, Dr. Fred Banting and assistant Charles Best worked on the diabetes mystery, in a hot, dingy laboratory and an even hotter operating room two more flights up, next door to the animal cages. Charley, and sometimes Fred, did all the cleaning, watering, feeding (the University's brand of dog food smelled vile), and dog fetching in rooms that often felt like an oven and smelled like a barn.

They tried to ignore the surroundings, as they led or carried dogs too sick to walk up and down the steps. Sometimes they harmonized old favorite songs as they tested blood, using up-to-date procedures which involved mixing small blood samples with chemicals, spinning them in a centrifuge, filtering, evaporating and drying them to find out how much sugar a dog's blood contained. Charley, the tall, blue-eyed, and handsome team chemist, could measure exactly how severely diabetic a dog was at any time. Fred had improved his surgical techniques.

Between experiments, the two went on picnics and dated. Other nights, they cooked eggs or steak in the lab, over a Bunsen burner. Charley, twenty-two, was engaged to a young woman who lived nearby. Fred's long-time engagement was off, then on, then off again.

More operations went wrong. More dogs died. The seven "duct-tied" dogs all turned up failures. The sutures had dissolved. Each dog's pancreas looked as healthy as ever.

All they could do was try again. Finally, a few procedures "went right."

By the end of July, the pair managed the "first step" toward solving the mystery. They removed the pancreas from one of their new duct-tied dogs. Fred felt a thrill of success. This time, the organ had degenerated. It looked grayish and ugly—definitely abnormal.

Fred carefully sliced the withered pancreas into thin sections and mashed them up with sand in an ice-cold Ringer's solution made of salts and water. He and Charley chilled the gritty mash, strained out the sand, filtered it, and warmed the cloudy result to dog-body temperature. Then they injected 4 cc. (about a tablespoon) into a small white diabetic terrier. The dog's blood sugar went down, then stayed steady, then inched back up, as they injected three more doses of pancreatic extract.

They fed the dog sugared water. Its blood sugar rose—but not by much. The experiment, so far, was a partial success. Pancreatic extract did have some effect. Major clue #1! The next morning, the little dog died.

They tried again, with a collie already almost dead from diabetes. The extract worked. The blood sugar went down. The dog even felt strong enough to stand up. Then it died.

Just to be sure, Fred tried the same experiments with extracts from spleen and liver. No other extract had any effect at all.

Slowly, one injection at a time, they built a string of successes. Their extract could bring down the high blood sugar level in diabetic dogs—most of the time. It could even lower the normal sugar level in normal dogs—part of the time. Nothing was certain.

Fred knew, in his own mind, that his project was a success. The extract worked—sometimes. What he needed to do, next, was keep a dog alive long enough to prove it. Meanwhile, he wrote to Dr. Macleod frequently, to explain his progress.

A week after Fred removed the pancreas on dog #92, the yellow collie was alive and almost healthy. "Frisky," Fred called her. She liked to put her head in his lap. The injections of pancreatic extract had to be keeping her alive.

Then disaster struck. They ran out of degenerated pancreas. Making more would take weeks, and Frisky could not live that long without it. Fred and Charley decided to experiment with whole pancreas. They tried one injection.

The first results looked good, but too many researchers had tried whole pancreas and failed. Fred didn't dare give the collie a second dose.

In an effort to save their favorite dog, they tried cat pancreas, from a cat whose duct they had tied only a week or so before. Dog #92 seemed to survive all their frantic efforts. She was still alive the following day. But cats are much smaller than collies. Again, they ran out of extract.

Next, they tried a new and complicated technique. A body hormone called secretin was known to stimulate the pancreas to make digestive juice. Maybe if they super-stimulated the pancreas, they could "wear it out." Maybe then it would stop making digestive juice, and they could get some of the mystery secretion quickly, without waiting weeks for the pancreas to atrophy. They tried the procedure on a cat.

The new extract worked. Dog #92 felt so well she jumped

out of her cage and ran around the room. Fred and Charley felt like jumping around the room, themselves. Success. A faster method and a new clue.

They tried a second time, using a second cat. This time, something went wrong. The cat died during the stimulation procedure. They used its pancreas, anyway.

When they injected the newest extract into Frisky, she went into shock. "When that dog died," Fred Banting wrote later, "the tears [fell] despite anything I could do." Fred went for a fast drive in his open Ford, calling it "a relief to be away and free."

A few days later, Professor Macleod returned. The scattering of good results pleased him, but he wanted better proof. Much better proof.

Macleod advised Banting and Best to redo all the same experiments, more carefully. They must be able to demonstrate, absolutely, that the lowered blood sugars they kept getting were due to their extract and not to any other factor. Maybe they were just diluting the blood. Macleod secretly wondered if they had actually proved anything at all.

Bad feelings broke out. Macleod and Banting argued over rooms (Fred wanted a better, cleaner laboratory), money (Macleod didn't want to spend any), and dogs (too many had died). Grudgingly, they compromised on a bigger room, the same amount of money, and more dogs.

Most important, the University of Toronto found a paying job for Dr. Fred Banting, as a "special lecturer" making, according to his biographer Michael Bliss, $250 per month. He earned less than Charley, his student assistant, but some money is better than none at all. Fred celebrated. Then he got back to work.

The team redid everything, relying most on the faster, superstimulation technique. Unfortunately, it worked only part of the time. More dogs and cats and even one calf died.

Fred injected Ringer's solution into several diabetic dogs, to show that the salty liquid, by itself, did not lower their blood sugar. Simply diluting the blood was not what made their extract work. He could prove it, now, to Dr. Macleod's satisfaction. But what *did* make their extract work?

Fred began to jot down his ideas on index cards, doing most of his thinking in the middle of the night. He soon had piles of cards. He and Charley began to search all the articles they could find on past experiments dealing with diabetes, reading about failure after failure. Fred wondered what to try next.

Macleod advised Fred to take the next major step: make a dog diabetic and see how long it could be kept alive. Only a long-living diabetic dog would prove the extract worked.

At the time, in mid-November, Fred had only one duct-tied dog on hand. Producing enough extract to treat a dog for a long period of time would take lots more surgery and months of waiting for pancreases to degenerate. The overstimulation method had not worked well enough. Fred needed a new shortcut.

On his index cards, Fred had jotted down some fresh clues. One looked especially important. Pregnant animals that lose their pancreas do not become diabetic until after their litters are born. Somehow, the mother draws the mystery substance directly from her babies. The idea hit Fred like a thunderbolt, at two in the morning. Maybe he could extract the mystery substance from fetuses.

Fred, who had grown up on a farm, remembered that

ranchers often breed their cows before sending them to market, to make them heavier. He and Charley set out for the nearest slaughterhouse. They bought nine calf fetuses, removed the tiny pancreas from each, and chopped them up in an icy dish of Ringer's solution.

Fred injected the filtered extract of calf pancreas into a diabetic dog. One day, and several injections later, the dog's blood sugar was almost normal. Its urine tested sugar-free.

Fred had stumbled onto the most vital clue so far. Unborn-calf extract worked. Since calf fetuses were easily available, that meant no more duct-tying on dogs. It meant no more pancreas-stimulating on cats. They could start fresh. Banting called his discovery the start of "a new era."

For the first time, they had plenty of pancreas to work with. Now they could try different ways to make the extract, looking for the best. Meanwhile, they started dog #27, whose pancreas had been removed November 14, on a longevity trial. How many days or weeks or months could they keep her alive?

The answer opened a new mystery. After two weeks of success, dog #27 went into convulsions and died. Something had gone wrong. The extract which had been keeping her alive seemed to have poisoned her. No one knew why.

Right away they chose a new dog, that had lost her pancreas on November 18. Hoping for the best, they gave her a name. Dog #33 (the numbers jump around) became Marjorie.

Fred and Charley both knew they needed a better way to make the extract. Sometimes their injections worked, sometimes they didn't, and sometimes they killed! What could they change? They reviewed the clues:

One, the extract could not have any pancreatic digestive juice in it, or the mystery substance disappeared. At least, that was what they had always heard. Two, it could not be heated, or, again, the substance disappeared. That, they had proved themselves.

To get around those problems, the team had tried degenerated pancreas and fetal pancreas, to eliminate the juice. To eliminate heating (other researchers boiled their solutions dry) they had evaporated water from the Ringer's solvent by gently blowing warm air across shallow dishes, a technique that Macleod had shown them. It was slow and troublesome, but it worked.

Now they decided to try alcohol. Alcohol evaporates much faster than water, and it seemed to dissolve the mystery substance just as well. Injections of the new extract, made from fetal calf pancreas ground up in alcohol, filtered, dried gently by air, and redissolved in Ringer's solution, brought Marjorie's blood sugar level down to normal.

Suddenly, Fred had another exciting idea. The other researchers who had tried to dissolve whole, adult pancreas in alcohol, had always boiled off the liquid. No one had ever taken as much trouble as they did to chill every step of the process. Maybe heat, not just the pancreatic juice, had been destroying the active ingredient.

Fred had a fresh dog pancreas he had just removed from a dog he was making diabetic. Instead of throwing the organ away, he made extract from it, using the new alcohol, low-temperature method.

They tried it on dog #35, not wanting to risk Marjorie. They watched carefully. No convulsions. No bad reaction. They drew blood and tested it. The sugar level had dropped drastically.

It worked! For the first time ever, Fred and Charley had made an effective extract from a normal adult pancreas. No more tiny fetuses! They had found the most important clue of all. They could use any pancreatic tissue available from any slaughterhouse (usually sold as "sweetbreads," a name for internal organ meat which some people like to eat). They had opened another "new era."

Now, the work needed speed. All over the world, people were still dying from the killer disease. Fred and Charley admitted they could use some help.

Dr. J.B. Collip, a biochemist at a nearby hospital, already had asked to join in the work. Charley felt a little shoved aside when a Ph.D. chemist took over, but he couldn't do everything that needed doing, quickly enough. Maybe Collip could.

The first few times Collip tried to duplicate Fred and Charley's extract, he failed. No effect. "There is something wrong with this whole piece of work," he announced, barging into Fred's lab.

Fred bristled. A scientist's work is no good if other people can't get the same results. He had to solve this minimystery quickly, or no one would believe in his discovery.

Like a detective, he retraced Collip's steps. Fred and Charley worked their way backwards through every procedure until they found themselves at the starting point—the slaughterhouse. Collip had found a different meat plant, closer to his lab at the hospital. There, all they had to do was listen.

When Collip sent his lab assistant to the slaughterhouse to buy "sweetbreads," he never bothered to specify what kind. "Sweetbreads" can mean several different kinds of organ meat, and each time, the butchers at the new place had given him a packet of thyroid and thymus glands. They sold every pancreas they collected separately to a fertilizer plant. Laughing about how ridiculous the pompous Dr. Collip looked when he found out, made Charley feel better.

But using mostly rabbits instead of dogs, Collip moved from his false start to rapid progress. By the end of December, he was making a potent extract and collecting solid evidence on how well it worked.

By the end of January, Collip had found ways to remove most of the impurities in the extract. Then late one night, tinkering with different solutions, Collip found that a 90-plus percent concentration of alcohol could actually make the mystery substance precipitate, or "fall out" of solution, into soft brown lumps at the bottom of the flask. Collip called his finding "the greatest thrill which has ever been given to me." He had actually seen the mystery substance, which came to be called insulin.

Meanwhile, over in Fred and Charley's lab, Marjorie still lived. (She lived seventy days, far longer than any other diabetic animal ever had.) The skeptics were astonished. They had to admit the mystery had been solved, as far as laboratory researchers could solve it.

Turning a laboratory experiment into a safe and effective drug for humans is never simple. Developing insulin as a treatment for diabetes took twice as long as making the discovery and involved the efforts of the whole University of Toronto science department, Eli Lilly & Company Pharmaceuticals, Toronto General Hospital, and a large number of other institutions and people. Eventually, it worked.

By 1923, insulin was widely available as a treatment for the deadly disease. Patients who had been given only weeks to live began to restart their lives. And also in 1923, Dr. Fred G. Banting and Dr. J.J.R. Macleod received Nobel Prizes for the discovery of insulin.

Angered because Best wasn't included and Macleod was, Fred immediately divided his share of the Nobel money with Charley. Macleod immediately divided his with Collip. The four had already spent the past months arguing over credit and who-did-what-and-when. The prize made the whole controversy worse.

Everyone agreed that Fred Banting deserved to be called the discoverer of insulin. He thought of the project and he carried it through.

People disagreed about Professor Macleod. To some, he received a Nobel Prize for work done while he was on vacation. Others feel he helped and guided Banting as a co-discoverer. Also, the director of a laboratory traditionally earns credit for any discoveries made in it.

People disagreed about Charles Best. Banting called him an equal partner in the discovery. Others don't believe graduate students should share in the awards their work brings. As for Collip, he arrived after the main discovery, but he took over the chemistry and delivered the necessary proof that Banting had not managed to provide. The arguments may never completely die.

But even an on-going controversy can't take away from the importance of the discovery Banting and the others made. Insulin revolutionized the treatment of a once deadly disease. It has saved and is still saving millions of lives.

# 8

# THE BROWN BEAN MYSTERY

The mystery began centuries ago in a slave-trading port in West Africa. Prisoners on trial for witchcraft were forced to eat a large, shiny brown seed called the Calabar bean, as a test of innocence. Most of the suspected "witches" clutched at their throats, gasped for breath, and died.

Trial judges thought the Calabar bean could determine guilt. Why else did some who ate it live and the rest die? Why else did victims sweat so profusely that their clothing became soaked? Why else did their throats close and their hearts stop beating? The deadly bean started a three-part mystery which baffled chemists for decades, until the grandson of an African slave found the final answer—in a test tube in Indiana.

Modern scientists quickly solved the easy part of the mystery. The hull of the bean contains a powerful emetic, causing victims to vomit violently. A lucky few prisoners managed to rid their systems of the whole bean at once. They lived.

The rest died. Inside a Calabar bean's tough, indigestible skin hides a deadly poison known as eserine. One bean contains enough to kill a dozen or more victims.

Next, chemists tackled eserine. What causes its deadly actions? Scientists found that it moves through the body, seeking and destroying a vital enzyme known as acetylcholinesterase. The body needs acetylcholinesterase to "reset the system," each time a nerve delivers a message, like the rewind button on a video machine. Without it, some nerves stop altogether, while others work overtime—exactly what happens when a victim bites down on a Calabar bean.

The second part of the mystery was barely solved before doctors saw a fabulous use for eserine, which chemists had renamed physostigmine (phy-sos-tiǵ-meen). Suppose the poison could be used, in carefully measured doses, to help patients paralyzed or in a coma when their bodies produced too much acetylcholinesterase. It might have other uses as well. Physostigmine could become a valuable drug.

Testing showed that physostigmine worked especially well in treating glaucoma, a serious eye disease which often led to blindness. Doctors and patients clamored for the exciting new chemical.

Demand caused a new problem. Physostigmine is found only in Calabar beans, and Calabar vines mainly grow along the Calabar River in Nigeria. Drug companies could not get enough beans to manufacture the drug. They needed a closer and cheaper source.

What they really needed was a way to manufacture physostigmine in the laboratory. The only trouble was, no one could figure out how to do it. When Percy Lavon Julian stumbled upon the mystery, in Vienna, Austria, some of the world's top chemists had already tried and given up.

Percy Julian's whole life, so far, had been a series of hopeless-looking mysteries. Brains, hard work and a little luck had solved them, one by one. Now he felt ready for a mysterious new challenge.

Percy's quest started in 1909, in a tree outside the white high school in Montgomery, Alabama. The young boy could see through an open window into the chemistry lab, where students seemed to be doing fascinating things with test tubes and beakers and bottles of chemicals. Percy decided right then that he wanted to be a chemist.

Before long, a policeman ordered him out of the tree. Small black boys were not allowed even to watch what went on in the white high school, much less study there.

The only black high school in Alabama had no test tubes, no beakers, no lab at all. Besides, it was miles away in Birmingham. Finding a way to become a chemist looked like a real mystery. Instead, Percy went to a local black teachers' college, graduating with top honors.

But Percy still wanted to be a chemist. He applied to DePauw University, in Greencastle, Indiana. Working double at his studies (he had to take so many remedial courses, it was almost like taking high school on top of college) as well as working at a full-time job, Percy Julian graduated at the head of his class—valedictorian and Phi Beta Kappa. Hard work and brains had solved one mystery. He was a chemist. But now what?

Most chemists graduating high in their class are awarded fellowships to graduate school. No school wanted Percy.

Dean William Blanchard advised him to get a job teaching at

a black college and forget about all the chemical mysteries he wanted to solve. He took the job, but he didn't forget.

When Harvard University offered a competition for the Austin Fellowship in chemistry, Percy entered and won. At Harvard, he earned his Masters' in one year, again at the top of his class. Still no serious fellowship offers. Brains and hard work still weren't enough. Percy went back to teaching.

Then good luck came through again. A classmate of Percy's appealed to his wealthy father, a member of the Rockefeller Foundation. They located a fellowship for Percy to study at the University of Vienna, in Austria, under Dr. Ernst Spath.

In Europe, the professors and other students hardly seemed to notice that Percy was black. Dr. Spath invited the young American to live at his house. While earning his Ph.D., Percy stumbled upon the Calabar bean mystery.

German scientists had been trying to "build" molecules of physostigmine by using raw materials found in soy beans. Soy beans, long a food staple in China, had in their chemical makeup, the "building blocks" for making a wide assortment of new and different chemicals. Percy Julian found the idea fascinating.

The whole thing was just the kind of mystery he had been looking for. He planned to be the first chemist to synthesize, or "make," physostigmine in the laboratory. But how? Soy beans might be the first clue.

Unfortunately, no one seemed to be having much luck. The soy bean included such a complex assortment of chemicals that it took everyone's time and energy just trying to sort them out.

Meanwhile, the physostigmine molecule turned out to have an incredibly confusing structure. Scientists had figured out enough clues to know its chemical formula:

$$C_{15} H_{21} N_3 O_2$$

but they weren't certain just how those forty-one atoms of carbon, hydrogen, nitrogen, and oxygen fit together. The molecule appeared to have three rings of atoms, attached side by side. And naturally, the whole molecule was much too small to see, even under a microscope. Physostigmine was a mystery.

Dr. Percy Julian took the mystery home to the United States with him in 1931, to a new job as a full professor at Howard University, in Washington, D.C. The most-respected black school in the country, Howard had a well-equipped lab (which Percy had helped establish a few years before), and the university even paid for two of Percy's classmates from Vienna to come and work as his assistants.

The three chemists began looking for clues. They took real physostigmine, extracted from the shiny brown beans, apart chemically, to explore ways to put it back together. The first clue they found "hit" them right in the nose—a chemical called indole.

Indole is a colorless solid which, when highly diluted, has a fragrant smell like the aroma of jasmine or orange blossoms. Indole, undiluted, gives raw sewage a major part of its stench.

Its formula, Percy Julian knew, is $C_8 H_7 N$. Indole has two attached rings of atoms, which chemists draw:

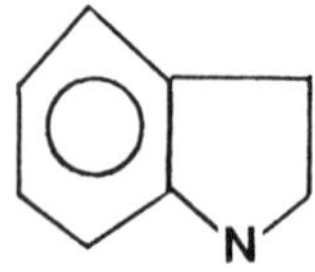


The hexagon shape with a circle inside is chemical shorthand for a ring of six carbon atoms, locked together, each attached to one hydrogen atom: Chemists call it a benzene ring.

The pentagon shape means a five-atom ring—four carbons and one nitrogen, the other atoms attached to atoms of hydrogen. Chemists call it a pyrrole ring. These two chemical rings, attached by sharing one "side" (two carbon atoms), make indole. And the double-ringed indole shape is the heart of the structure of physostigmine.

A molecule's shape, Percy Julian knew, can sometimes matter more than the atoms inside, when a chemist is trying to "build" molecules from scratch. But with indole, he had both—the right basic shape, made out of the right atoms. Now, all he had to do was get the right sorts of other atoms attached.

The idea of any chemical synthesis is to take a basic building block identical to one part of the target substance and then add other "blocks" of atoms to it, by using a thorough knowledge of the way different chemicals act. Only skilled and clever chemists are able to keep all the clues straight. "Chemical cunning," some people call the knack for synthesis. Percy Julian wanted to prove he had it.

Before Dr. Julian and his two assistants got too far, a crisis interrupted their work. Howard University was oriented toward teaching, not research. The rest of the faculty thought the three chemists ought to give up their efforts on the physostigmine mystery and spend more time teaching chemistry.

Percy Julian appealed to his favorite professor, Dean Blanchard, at DePauw. Dr. Blanchard not only invited his former student back to DePauw, he personally raised the money to fund the research, so work on the physostigmine mystery could go on. "It must go on," Blanchard said. Patients with glaucoma were still going blind for lack of the medicine they needed.

As soon as he could wrap things up, Percy moved back to Indiana. One assistant, Dr. Josef Pikl, went with him.

By 1934, they had assembled a lab full of clues. In soy beans, for instance, they located a chemical called tryptophan, a building block of protein which has the indole double ring, with a long chain of extra atoms sticking off one corner. Maybe, they reasoned, that chain could be bent into a third ring.

Day after day the two chemists, along with six students assigned to help them, worked over the sometimes flowery, sometimes foul-smelling chemicals. They stirred and dissolved and melted and recrystallized test tubes of colorless crystals, lemon-yellow crystals, and beautiful blood-red crystals. They added alcohols and acids, stirred in palladium, sodium, bubbles of hydrogen gas. They boiled strong-smelling solutions for hours and then chilled them in ice.

Since the exact structure of physostigmine was still partly a mystery, the crew had to stop at each step in their synthesis and prove that what they thought they had in the test tube was really what they had.

Part of the time, they worked forward, building up molecules by using chemicals they extracted from soy beans. Orange blossoms, when they could get them, turned out to be an even better source. So did coal tar. Part of the time, they worked backwards, carefully dividing extracts from Calabar beans into smaller chemical units.

The rest of the time, they worked in the middle, comparing real parts to synthetic parts, piece by invisible piece and crystal by crystal. Then disaster struck, again. The money ran out.

Everything Dr. Blanchard had collected had been spent, and DePauw had no further money to spare.

Percy felt ready to give up. People had been telling him for years that a black man could never be a serious chemist, and he finally began to wonder if they were right. He joked that it might be time to "start making an honest living driving a truck."

Then luck, added to brains and hard work, changed the gloomy picture. The Rosenwald Foundation, a private fund interested in education of black people, took an interest in Dr. Julian's work. They donated enough money to keep the laboratory running at least one more year.

The team of chemists had barely had time to relax from the financial crisis, when a different disaster loomed. Sir Robert Robinson, head of the chemistry department at Oxford University, in England, published an article declaring that he had synthesized the chemical precursors to physostigmine. He was, he wrote, almost ready to put the complete molecule together.

In science, the person who announces a discovery first—the one who "solves the mystery"—almost always gets the credit. Three years of hard work might all be for nothing! Percy Julian read Dr. Robinson's paper with a large knot in the pit of his stomach.

Halfway through the article, he began to relax. The British chemist's part-molecules, which proposed to lead to physostigmine, were nothing like the ones Percy and his crew had built. Not even close. The method—and the results—were totally different.

Robinson had to be wrong. All wrong. He had missed every

clue. Percy began to feel better. He would write an article of his own, he said, outlining the *right* steps to synthesizing physostigmine.

Then his friends pointed out a horrible possibility. Suppose, just suppose, Robinson turned out to be right. Suppose Percy wrote an article disagreeing with the famous Oxford professor and then Robinson synthesized physostigmine first.

Scientists choose the "wrong path" toward important discoveries all the time, and no one thinks worse of them. But a black chemist, in 1934, could not afford to be wrong. If he made himself look stupid in print, his short research career would be over. It would be back to teaching at small black colleges forever.

Percy hesitated. Then he made up his mind. He knew his results were correct, and he was willing to stake his career on them.

Percy and Pikl mailed an article to the *Journal of the American Chemical Society* outlining their work. "We believe the English authors are in error," they wrote, describing a precursor chemical of their own as "the real" step on the way to success.

Then they threw a direct challenge to Dr. Robinson. "We shall prove the correctness of our position definitely with the complete and final synthesis of physostigmine," Percy wrote. The race to the mystery's solution was on.

After that, the team worked even longer hours in the lab. Chemical followed chemical. Crystalline "bundles of needles," as Percy described them, separated into saltlike grains, which dissolved in acetone (a chemical often used as nail polish remover). More chemical steps led to more clear and colorful crystals.

Then things bogged down. One important procedure resulted in a thick, tarry glue stuck to the inside of a glass flask. Nothing could get it all out.

Backing up, they tried the step again. Same result. Prolonged heating could melt off a little, but most of the chemical they needed clung like black gum to the inside of the glass.

Finally, someone got a brilliant idea. Maybe they remembered making taffy, or maybe one of the chemists thought about Charles Goodyear (see "The Sticky Secret") and his efforts with rubber. Anyway, the group tried pouring out the hot chemical onto a marble slab. Boiling hot, it all came sliding out of the flask at once. It cooled into a dark, solid lump on the cool slab. They beat it into chunks with a hammer and went on.

Finally, at ten o'clock, on a February night in 1935, the final product was ready. A pinch of colorless crystals represented the end result. Physostigmine salt, as pure as any made from African brown beans. At least, they hoped that's what they had.

The final proof would be the crystals' melting point. Natural physostigmine salt melts at exactly 139° C. The slightest difference between their product and the real thing would throw off the melting point. Even one misplaced hydrogen atom would raise or lower the temperature a noticeable amount.

Percy Julian carefully transferred a few crystals to a tiny glass test tube, made by hand from a hollow glass rod. It held a line of tiny crystals so thin that it would melt all at once, the instant the glass reached their melting point.

His assistant placed a few grains of natural physostigmine in a similar tube. Then they each fastened their tiny test tube to a thermometer immersed in a large beaker of fluid.

Gradually they heated the bath, in which both tubes sat. The crystals didn't change, as the temperature slowly climbed.

Each man watched his own tube carefully. They both knew measuring a melting point requres keeping the eyes constantly on the tiny crystals. One glance away can mean missing the crucial point.

Professor Blanchard, sitting in the lab, watched the thermometer, both tubes, and both men. No one moved, as the temperature reading neared 139°.

Then the room erupted. "I'm melting!" Percy Julian shouted. "Me, too!" yelled Josef Pikl. The crystals in both tubes had turned to liquid at exactly the same moment, at exactly the same temperature—139°, the melting point of the natural salt of physostigmine.

The three men jumped up and threw their arms around each other. The final mystery was solved.

The synthesis of artificial physostigmine won praise from scientists all over the world. Dr. Percy L. Julian won a number of prizes, including (in 1947) the Spingarn Medal of the National Association for the Advancement of Colored People for "brilliant contributions in the field of chemical research," and several honorary degrees. He even found time, later in 1935, to marry Anna Johnson, a research sociologist with her own Ph.D.

Unfortunately, none of the honors Dr. Julian won could overcome prejudice against a black professor at a white university. Even DePauw turned him down. Instead, he took a job in industry, as head of the soy bean research department at the Glidden Company.

Within a few years, Percy Julian had turned Glidden's losses into profits, synthesized male and female hormones and the anti-arthritis drug cortisone from soy beans, created fire-fighting foam, started his own company and made himself into a millionaire. From African beans to a tree in Alabama to a test tube in Indiana to a multimillion-dollar industry, the physostigmine mystery made life better for millions of people, but especially for chemist Percy Lavon Julian.

# 9

# THE CASE OF THE JUMPING GENES

In the Pink Panther movies, Inspector Clouseau could never communicate his discoveries to anyone around him. Bumbling through Europe, he always seemed to be speaking a language no one else understood. Clouseau solved his cases alone because other people thought he was crazy.

Dr. Barbara McClintock worked alone, too, in a lab and a cornfield in New York. Barbs McClintock never "bumbled," but, like Clouseau, she seemed to speak a language all her own. Few biologists ever understood what she was talking about. "That woman is either crazy or a genius," one scientist announced. But which?

Staring at a white leaf from a mutant, or abnormal, cornstalk she had planted, Barbara McClintock spotted some dark green streaks. She knew she had uncovered a mystery—the second big one of her career.

The whole plant looked streaked and blotchy. In fact, so did every cornstalk in the field. Most people would not have seen anything special about these particular streaks. But Barbs wasn't "most people." And she knew more about Indian corn than anyone else in the world.

When Eleanor McClintock was only four months old, in 1902, her mother changed her name to Barbara. Mrs. McClintock thought the spunky baby looked far too independent for a "feminine" name like Eleanor.

Barbs carried her independent spirit to New York's Cornell University, where she earned a degree in botany, the study of plants. Shedding her heavy skirts for a pair of trousers she had specially made, Barbara McClintock spent most of her time out in a cornfield. The waving cornstalks sometimes towered over her barely five-foot-high head, but already Barbs had discovered what she loved most. Even more than running on the beach or playing a jazz banjo, she loved uncovering the secrets of maize, the colorful, speckled, variegated ears of Indian corn.

Indian corn seemed full of mystery. Why were some kernels deep purple and others pale? Where did the bronze and rose and magenta hues come from? And how did each kernel know what color to become? Barbara didn't know, but she intended to find out.

Trying to enroll in graduate school dealt Barbs a setback. Even at Cornell, which emphasized "any person in any study," women were not allowed to study plant breeding. Too unfeminine. Too "unsuitable."

She got around the problem by ignoring it. Barbara McClintock earned her Ph.D. in botany, majoring in cytology (the study of cells) and minoring in genetics (the study of heredity)—which amounted to the same thing as plant breeding, as long as she didn't call it that.

Her degree didn't make much difference, anyway. No one offered her a job. No jobs existed for women scientists in 1927, except teaching at a girls' school. Barbs had no intention of spending her life explaining the parts of a plant to a room full of giggling students. She wanted to solve scientific mysteries.

Barbs already knew what mystery she wanted to solve first—Mendel's mystery. She wanted to prove how parents pass traits along to their offspring.

In the 1860s, an Austrian monk named Gregor Johann Mendel crossed plants having green seeds with plants having yellow seeds, to see what would happen. Yellow seeds happened. Then he crossbred the yellow-seeded results. Three out of four plants again grew yellow seeds. The others produced green.

Mendel interbred purple-flowered peas with white-flowered peas, smooth peas with wrinkled peas, and even tall pea plants with short pea plants—thirty-four different kinds. Every time, he found a predictable mathematical pattern to the way their offspring developed.

Some unit—Mendel didn't know what—seemed to "carry" traits and characteristics down through the generations of plants. Traits such as wrinkles or green color could hide and then show up, mysteriously, several generations later.

Mendel wrote a paper about his discoveries, but no one paid much attention. It was full of mathematical formulas, and biologists of his day didn't deal in math. No one understood what Mendel was talking about.

Almost fifty years later, just about the time Barbara McClintock was born, a new generation of scientists discovered

Mendel's paper. His ideas began to make more sense.

By then, biologists had improved their microscopes and could see what happened when cells divide in two. During cell division, some short strings from the center of the cell stretch out and begin to sort themselves into two sets. Half go into each developing cell. The mysterious strings, looking, as one scientist has described it, "like a tangle of stubby spaghetti," help to form the new cell's nucleus.

Cells are mostly transparent, but when biologists added special kinds of dye to their dividing specimens, they could see the "spaghetti" more clearly than any other part of the cell. In fact, the tangled filaments absorbed dye so well that they came to be called "chromosomes," from the Greek word for "color." But in nondividing cells, they barely showed up at all.

Obviously, chromosomes become important when cells divide. Biologists suspected they had something to do with inherited traits. Could they carry the mysterious units Mendel had described? No one knew how to find out.

Barbara McClintock loved looking at chromosomes. Peering through her microscope at the brightly colored tangle, she felt as if she were meeting friends. According to her biographer, Evelyn Fox Keller, in *A Feeling for the Organism*, she got to know each one of maize's ten chromosomes "personally."

Barbs quickly learned to recognize each chromosome by size and shape (which almost got her fired from her after-school job as a cytologist's assistant. Her boss had been working for months, trying to find a way to tell the tiny chromosomes apart. Adapting a new cell-staining technique she had heard about, Barbs quickly did what he could not. He was not pleased).

Scientists had already given Mendel's units a name, "genes," meaning "to produce." But did genes really exist? That was Mendel's mystery.

If they existed, someone needed to find them. Barbs—now Dr. McClintock—set to work on the problem.

Most work in genetics, in the 1920s, had been done on a tiny bug known as *Drosophila melanogaster,* the fruit fly. Working with *Drosophila* provided several big advantages over corn. Fruit flies have only four chromosomes per cell. They are cheap and easy to grow. Also, they hatch a new generation every ten days, while one corn crop takes a whole year. New clues came fast.

One team of scientists had just published a book which almost—but not quite—proved that genes on the chromosomes of fruit flies carry eye color and wing shape information from one generation to the next. The trouble was, the actual *Drosophila* chromosomes were too tiny to see in any detail, even under the best microscopes available.

Holding a tiny bug under a microscope to check for red eyes did not appeal to Barbs. She liked the solid, satisfying feel of an ear of maize, with its row of multicolored kernels.

She also like the pace, with a whole winter in which to examine and think about each new generation. Slower clues, but clearer. She decided to look for evidence of genes in corn.

Barbs had a new approach to the mystery in mind. Geneticists had been breeding swarms of *Drosophila*, looking for clues to genes. Cytologists had been pouring over the super-tiny fruit fly cells, looking for the same thing. No one person was looking both places. And nobody was looking at maize.

For two years, Barbs followed her generations of corn, carefully examining each ear both by hand and under the microscope. She filled notebooks with careful descriptions of each kernel on each cob and each chromosome in each cell.

One of the new graduate students, Harriet Creighton, became her assistant. Sometimes lunching right in the field to save time, Barbs and Harriet harvested the third year's corn. In the evening, they spent the extra time playing tennis.

Later, in the lab, they examined ear after ear, cell after cell. Through the microscope's eyepiece, they could see the ten tangled chromosomes, all different sizes and shapes, all with tiny lumps and bumps and branches.

Staining plant cells with dye kills the individual cell, but it wasn't hard to find different cells in each stage of the dividing process. The two young women, searching for clues, watched red-stained chromosomes rest, lengthen, stretch, double over or pair up, and separate.

After months of looking, Harriet and Barbs began to see the special clue Barbs had been looking for. The twisted chromosomes did not always look exactly alike, from one cell to another. They sometimes developed differences which could be seen; differences which could be followed from one generation to the next. For instance, some dark kernels' cells had a tiny extra knob on chromosome #9. Cells from light-colored kernels didn't.

The next crop got careful attention. Each kernel, as it buds, must be fertilized by pollen (which grows on the corn's tassel), of its own or from another plant. Barbs slid a paper bag over each small, developing ear, to protect it from stray pollen in the air. Harriet, much taller, put paper bags over the tassels at the top of the corn plants, to trap the pollen they wanted to collect.

With paintbrushes, they spread pollen grown from kernels

bearing the "extra knob" onto cornsilks from kernels that didn't have it, carefully cross-mating them. They watered and watched the growing stalks.

In the meantime, Barbs checked back through the earlier generations. Same situation. Each time, she could tell the color of a kernel, just by looking at its chromosomes under a microscope. No one had ever been able to do that before. She collected other, more complex evidence to back up her discovery.

The new generation checked out perfectly. Every kernel Barbs predicted would have a knob in its chromosomes had one. Every one that shouldn't, didn't.

Barbs could show proof that a real, physical change took place in chromosomes to match a real, physical change in an organism. Genes really existed. Mystery #1 was solved!

The paper Dr. McClintock and Harriet Creighton published has become a classic in genetics. It made Barbara McClintock semi-famous, in biological circles. Within a few years, it and other papers, got her elected vice-president—eventually president—of the Genetics Society of America and even a membership (one of the first three women) in the National Academy of Sciences.

But it still couldn't get her a research job. Women were expected to teach or work in their husband's lab, not do research of their own.

For the next few years, Barbs covered the country in her Model A Ford, working temporarily at several universities. She earned two short-term grants and even a fellowship in Germany. But when all that was over, she still had no job, no lab, and most important, no cornfield of her own.

A geneticist friend of Barbs' had just accepted a professorship at Columbia University in New York City. He specialized in maize, too. She wrote to ask where he planned to grow his corn.

He had an answer—Cold Spring Harbor Laboratory, tucked between the woods and Long Island Sound, not far from New York City. The labs were supported by the Carnegie Institution of Washington, which hired scientists to do research. Barbs drove there, planted her corn, spent the summer. The director liked her work. She spent the rest of her career there.

Now Barbs had "an oasis"—in an unheated garage across the road from the main laboratories. She had a cornfield. Time for a fresh mystery. But what? She decided to "ask the corn."

Every spring Barbs planted maize, using kernels from the strains she had been studying for years. Working with no assistants or technicians, she watered and fed the growing plants, protecting them from bugs and drought and stray baseballs from the diamond in the next field. She harvested the corn when it was ready and spent the winter analyzing each crop.

If Barbara had not known her corn so well, she might never have noticed Mystery #2. The first clue looked so unimportant most people would have paid no attention. She saw funny-looking dark streaks on a white leaf.

Geneticists frequently study mutations—the effects on an organism when chromosomes, or the genes on them, change in some way. X-rays can cause artificial mutations, or they can simply happen on their own.

Maize normally has a high mutation rate. That's what causes it to have the speckled, varigated colors so different from the pale yellow corn sold in grocery stores.

This year, 1944, Barbs wanted to study cell damage. She planted and self-pollinated about 450 kernels whose #9 chromosome usually broke. Broken chromosomes make "a genetic mess." Where and how, she wondered, would the damage show?

Certain genes on chromosome #9 control the color of each individual corn kernel, from pale yellow to vivid purple. Other genes control the shades of green and yellow and white on the leaves. Broken chromosomes usually produce spotted and unusual color patterns.

Barbs knew each kernel and each leaf grows from one single cell. If that cell is damaged, the damage must show up somewhere. She meant to find the evidence.

A cell damaged early, right at the start of a seed's growth, affects the whole plant. Cells whose chromosomes break later in the development may affect only one kernel or one leaf or one tiny spot on one leaf.

Some mysterious green streaks caught Barbara's eye. The whole crop showed signs of cell damage, but this one particular leaf was a puzzle. One part of the white leaf had a patchwork of dark green streaks, while the part right next to it had almost none. The second section, in fact, looked almost exactly like a "negative" of the first.

Barbara turned the new mystery over in her mind. "Thinking about things" had always been her hobby. Somewhere in the development of the leaf, a cell divided into two sister cells. One, Barbara decided, must have gained an extra "something"—and the other lost it. The first cell grew into a leaf segment with extra streaks. The second grew into a segment without.

The odd behavior looked "startlingly conspicuous" to her trained eye, even if no one else noticed. But what exactly had happened? And how?

Barbs forgot all about studying cell damage. This new mystery was much more interesting. She was sure she was looking at something very basic—and yet completely unknown to scientists. And she had discoverd it by accident.

If Barbara's ideas were right, her new mystery was clue to the biggest genetic mystery of all: how does each cell in an organism, having the same set of chromosomes as every other cell in the organism, know what to do? How do some cells in a corn plant know to turn into roots, others into leaves and still others into stalks and kernels and cobs and silk? How? No one had ever figured it out.

Barbara McClintock began to study every plant in her latest crop carefully, looking for other "twin" spots, where one area seemed to have gained what another lost. She found dozens. Kernels which ought to be pale were streaked with color, while "sister" kernels grew in just the opposite pattern. "Bizarre," Barbs called it. What was going on?

Barbs turned the cobs over and over in her hands, examining every part. The clue was no fluke. It existed. But what did it mean?

Barbara took out her glass slides and dyes. On the big slate table in the middle of her lab, she began to prepare samples from her corn, to examine under the microscope.

The next clue was not so obvious. Barbs needed all her years of experience to put the facts together. When she did, the answer astounded her. Some genes in the cell had moved to a new location. It was almost as if they had "jumped."

Barbara couldn't wait for spring. She planted forty kernels from each mysterious new ear in a greenhouse, to grow during the winter.

She watched the spring crop carefully as it grew. Some leaves had the mystery spots. Some didn't. Barbs could hardly wait to get the cells under her microscope.

The answer jumped out at her. If the moving gene stayed in its new location in the new crop, the new color pattern also stayed. But frequently, the "jumping genes" jumped back. Back came the original colors!

Jumping genes seemed to be able to turn color genes on and off like a switch, in kernels and leaves and everywhere. No one had ever noticed such a thing before.

Barbs had to learn more. Soon maize plants in pots were growing all around her office, in any available spot.

For two years, she collected and sorted and examined her data. By now, she had a pretty clear idea of what was happening. Moving genes could cause cells to do completely new things. They could give individual cells individual "orders." They could, in modern terms, "reprogram" themselves.

Meanwhile, Barbs was having a marvelous time tracking down the clues. "It was *fun*!" she said. "I couldn't wait to get up in the morning."

Her discovery didn't make conventional sense. "Everyone knew" genes sat on chromosomes like beads on a string. If a gene disappeared, from damage or whatever, it never came back.

But Barbara's "jumping genes" did. She named them "transposable elements," or "TE's." They could do amazing things, changing a whole generation of kernels from yellow to red, and the next one back to yellow, just by their position on the chromosome. Any time they moved, something changed.

Through her data, Barbs could follow the position of two TE's, which she called Ac, the Activator gene and Ds, the Dissociator. Ds "jumped," causing one kind of change if Ac happened to be nearby, and another kind if it weren't. Somehow, the Ac could send a signal to the Ds, causing it to move. Sometimes, when cells split, one "sister" got the jumping gene and the other didn't. The result: "twin" mutations.

Barbs planted more maize. It gave her more piles of data. More maize. More data. More fun for Barbs. Everything fit.

The results were difficult to follow. She had uncovered several kinds of TE's doing complicated things, but Barbs thought the whole genetics world would be as excited as she was. She published an article. No one paid much attention.

Barbara McClintock knew she was holding the answer to questions geneticists had been asking for decades. Moveable Ac and Ds genes explain how cells in a growing corn plant "know" whether to become kernels or leaves or parts of the stalk. They explain why certain mutations happen. They could explain the way cells respond to shock. Jumping genes probably, Barbs figured, even explain how a caterpiller turns into a butterfly.

For four more years, she collected data. Barbara planned to present the full details to her colleagues in an important 1951 seminar at Cold Spring Harbor.

As is customary at a scientific meeting, Dr. Barbara McClintock read her paper aloud. Most of the world's top biologists sat in the audience.

Barbara's speech bombed. Totally! No one asked questions.

No one even looked interested. "They thought I had flipped my top," she said later.

Barbara had been misunderstood before. She waited a few months and tried again. Still, no one cared about her "jumping genes" In fact, other geneticists thought she was crazy. Her ideas didn't fit with what "everyone knew" about genes. Her techniques sounded "old-fashioned." Her papers were too complicated to understand. No one bothered.

Barbara stopped publishing articles. Why go to all that trouble, she thought, when no one wants to read them, anyway.

Some scientists might have given up entirely. Mendel did, when the same thing happened to him. He transferred his energy to church work and grew too fat to bend over in the garden.

Not Barbara McClintock. She didn't quit working or get fat. She just followed her regular routine—aerobics early in the morning, a walk in the woods or on the beach, work with maize for the rest of the day, and a final walk in the woods. Unsorted, unpublished data piled up in notebooks, stacked neatly in her office.

Barbara knew her scientific mystery—the mystery of how cells change—was solved, but she gave up trying to solve the harder mystery—getting people to listen. Her results were right. Sooner or later, everyone else would discover what she already knew. "It will all come out in the wash," Barbara told herself.

A mystery isn't officially solved when nobody believes the solution. For more than twenty years, Barbs' discovery just lay around, ignored.

The fashion had changed in genetics. No one was interested,

anymore, in working with plants or animals. Even fruit flies, with four chromosomes and a ten-day life cycle, seemed too complex.

Bacteria had everything the up-to-date geneticist needed: new generations in days or even hours; simple, single strand chromosomes, which the new electron microscopes could bring into sharp focus. Work with bacteria offered "quick returns."

Universities stopped bothering to teach classical genetics. No one was interested.

Then a pair of French biologists made an astonishing discovery. Sections of genes in the bacteria they were studying seemed to move from place to place. Just as surprising, they seemed to be controlled by other sections of genes on the same chromosome. The two wrote a paper describing what they thought was a major discovery. Then they got the biggest surprise of all. The discovery had already been made.

Barbara's mystery had not been lost, just buried. Now, some thirty years since Barbara noticed the peculiar streaks on a leaf of her corn, her ideas made a lot more sense. Now, they fit perfectly with what other biologists were doing. Suddenly, Barbs' discovery was "in fashion." Geneticists everywhere began noticing "jumping genes."

"I had to psych myself up," she said, to deal with all the excitement. Barbs had been ignored too long to enjoy publicity now.

The scientific community wanted to make up for earlier rejections. Barbara McClintock received thousands of dollars in awards, from the McArthur Foundation, the Lasker Award, Israel's Wolf Foundation, and finally the Nobel Prize. (She was only the third woman ever to win a Nobel Prize in science alone—Marie Curie, see "The Secret in the Old Shed"—was first.)

Since their rediscovery, jumping genes have been found in every kind of organism tested. They may even be able to explain why blood makes antibodies against disease, why some cells become cancers, and why evolution progresses. Barbara McClintock single-handedly started a revolution in biology. It just took a while to get underway.

*rtesy, Goodyear*

CHARLES GOODYEAR.

*Aluminum Association,*

CHARLES M. HALL.

Original specimens of pure aluminum produced by Charles Martin Hall's electrolytic reduction process in 1886.

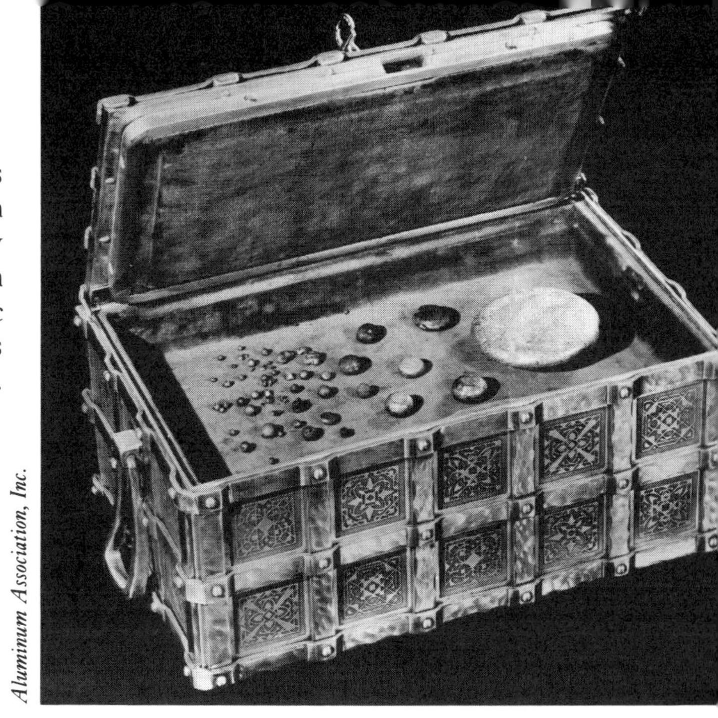

*Aluminum Association, Inc.*

An assistant, left, with Drs. Pierre and Marie Curie in her laboratory.

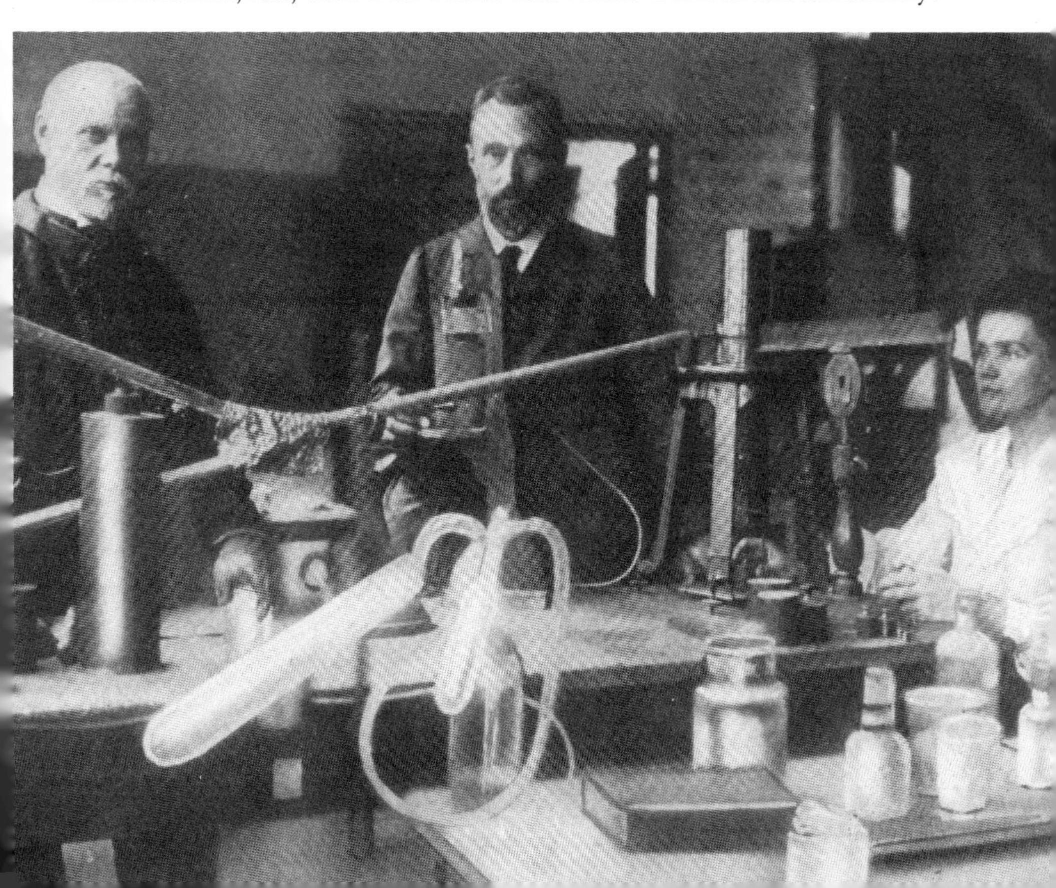

Courtesy, National Institute of Health, Rocky Mountain Laboratories

DR. HOWARD T. RICKETTS.

Pierre and Marie Curie on vacation, 1906.

DR. ERNEST RUTHERFORD.

*E.F. Smith Memorial Collection, Center for History of Chemistry, University of Pennsylvania*

*Library of Cong*

DR. NIELS BOHR.

DR. FRED BANTING.

*Faculty of Medicine, University of Toronto*

*Faculty of Medicine, University of Toronto*

DR. CHARLES BEST.

DR. PERCY L. JULIAN.
as a student at
DePauw University.

*Courtesy, DePauw University*

Cold Spring Laboratory, Photographer David Micklas

DR. BARBARA MCCLINTOCK.

PERCY L. JULIAN with his class at DePauw University, circa 1920.

Dr. Jack Kilby.

Courtesy, Texas Instruments

Courtesy, Fairchild Semiconductor Corporat

*rtesy, National Institute of Mental Health*

DR. CANDACE PERT.

DR. ROBERT NOYCE.

Courtesy, *Institute of Human Origins*

DR. DON JOHANSON AND "FRIEND."

Courtesy, *University of Houston*

DR. PAUL CHU.

# 10

# THE CASE OF THE INCREDIBLE SHRINKING CHIP

Rock and roll music blared through parks and beaches. "Top Forty" tunes vibrated faintly from the back rows of classrooms and study halls, especially if the teacher was a little hard-of-hearing. From Elvis Presley's "Blue Suede Shoes" to Pat Boone's "Tutti Frutti," popular songs followed teenagers of the late 1950s wherever they went. All anyone needed was one of the new, tiny transistor radios.

No longer did radios need to be large, expensive wooden boxes filled with fragile glass tubes. No longer did radios have to stay in the family living room. A new invention called the transistor made radios small and cheap and portable. People expected all sorts of fabulous new electronic gadgets to appear, now that scientists had "solved" the size mystery.

Most people didn't know a dark secret every engineer knew. The real mystery had not been solved. It was just beginning.

Experts called it "the numbers barrier"—a puzzle no one could solve. Electronic devices, from radios to computers (which, in the 1950s, filled whole rooms) could not get much smaller for two reasons: one physical and one practical.

First, electronic circuits—the "inside parts" which made a radio or a computer work—took up too much space. A radio was fairly simple, but the smallest computer needed thousands of circuits and millions of connecting wires—easily a roomful.

Second, the smaller engineers tried to make an individual circuit, the more difficult attaching wires to all its parts became. In other words, engineers in the 1950s could design all sorts of tiny devices on paper, but no one could actually build them. The "numbers barrier" was a major mystery, and a major block to progress.

All around the world, scientists and engineers had been working for years on the puzzle. First, they tried smaller glass tubes. The tubes burned out. They hired women with especially small hands to try and attach tiny wires under microscopes. Wires came loose.

Then they invented the transistor, a whole new technology where electricity moved through solid metal instead of vacuum tubes. Transistors could be made quite small, but they still needed hundreds and thousands and millions of hand-soldered wires, which took up too much space, cost too much money, and came unwired too often. Computers still filled huge rooms. Most ideas fell through. Nothing worked.

Jack St. Clair Kilby decided to solve the mystery. An engineer, Jack had already invented more than a dozen electronic tools, and he felt ready to try his personal "inventing method" on a bigger problem. But the small Wisconsin lab where he designed hearing aids didn't have the right facilities. Solving the barrier mystery might require some expensive materials and techniques. How could he get the necessary backing?

Jack mailed out a stack of résumés. He wanted, he wrote, to work on making electronic circuits smaller. He hoped to experiment with a "new" material he had read about called silicon. Texas Instruments, interested in both, offered him a job. Jack and his wife and two daughters moved from Milwaukee southwest to Dallas.

Then disappointment hit. T.I. signed a contract to work on the U.S. Army's new Micro-Modules, an idea for making circuits smaller. The plan involved building small, prewired circuits to be snapped together like interlocking beads. Jack felt sure he would be assigned to the project.

He also felt sure the Army's idea was all wrong. It couldn't possibly work. Had he moved all the way to Texas to waste energy on a doomed project?

Jack trusted his personal "inventing method." First and most important, he identified the problem. Jack called it "getting the picture." This step often turned out to be the hardest.

Then he learned every detail he could about the materials and procedures involved. Finally, he tried every possible solution, no matter how unlikely, until he hit on the right one. So far, the method had worked for him.

The Army, Jack thought, had already failed step one. They identified the wrong problem.

In scientific language, "micro" means "one-millionth," or anything "super-small." Jack knew "Micro-Modules" involved a new way to lock small, individual circuits together. Locking circuits together was not the biggest problem. How to *build* micro-circuits was the mystery. He had to find a solution.

That summer of 1958, T.I. required all employees to take vacation at the same time, in the first two weeks of July. With no vacation time coming, Jack Kilby, six-foot-six-inch newcomer to Texas, found himself working alone in a deserted plant.

Being alone suited Jack's work-style. He needed time to read and think about the "numbers barrier." If he could find a solution to the mystery before everyone got back, he could escape going to work on Micro-Modules. Jack Kilby began to sort out the clues.

Sitting alone in the cavernous T.I. plant, Jack reviewed everything he had ever learned about circuits—electric and electronic. Electricity deals with moving electrons, the super-tiny subatomic particles discovered by J.J. Thomson (see "The Case of the Astounding Rebound"), which make up the "outside" part of every atom. Electrons can jump from one atom to another, and as they do, they carry electricity.

An *electric circuit* refers to electrons flowing from a source around in a complete circle, back to the source. Electricity moves through a *conductor*, usually a metal wire.

As a kid, Jack had loved radios—not just listening, but sending messages. He earned his ham radio operator's license at fourteen, building his own set and learning about circuits and overheated tubes and burned-out wires the hard way.

Radios use electronic circuits. An *electronic circuit* means one where the electrons' movement is deliberately controlled or changed.

In a radio, for instance, Jack had learned to add *amplifiers*, to increase the current in his circuits and *resistors* to control that current (volume knobs are resistors), and *capacitors* to hold and release current (tuning knobs are capacitors). He had built *rectifiers* to control the direction of electron flow, *oscillators* to vary the current's direction, and *diodes* to turn it on and off.

These and other components, wired together, make up electronic circuits. Different components allow circuits to do different jobs, but not every circuit needs every kind.

Every component needs a special kind of material. Conductors are usually metal, which lets electrons move easily. Resistors are usually carbon (like the "lead" in a pencil), which stops electrons from moving. Capacitors may have two metal plates with carbon in-between.

Jack's ambition, to graduate from M.I.T., fell apart when he flunked the entrance exam. Twice. Then World War II interrupted his years at the University of Illinois, and Jack spent time in the Army—repairing radios.

The earliest electronic devices, from radios to computers, used glass vacuum tubes as rectifiers. Then transistors took over. Jack had been designing transistorized hearing aids back in Wisconsin, so he qualified as something of an early expert.

Transistors combined some of the features of an electronic circuit into one, using special materials called *semiconductors*—which could conduct electricity or hold it back, depending upon exactly how they were put together.

Germanium and silicon, both metal-like elements, act as semiconductors. Both are found in sand and rocks and dirt.

In a transistor, the same piece of germanium, "doped," or mixed with tiny bits of other elements, can conduct electrons one way on both ends and the reverse direction in the middle. It acts as a conductor on the ends and something like a resistor in-between.

Scientists named the new component a *transistor.* Transistors work far better than vacuum tubes; they don't burn out, they are smaller and cheaper, and they never need to "warm up" the way a tube does.

But for large jobs, huge numbers of transistors still had to be wired together. A mid-1950s computer needed thousands of transistors, four times as many other components, and millions of hand-wired connections which had to be, as one engineer put it, "made, tested, packed, shipped, unpacked, retested, and interconnected one-at-a-time." One loose wire shut down the whole thing.

Jack knew transistors didn't solve the barrier mystery. They only made it more frustrating.

Most transistors Jack had handled were made of germanium, which was easy to purify and to "dope" with whatever extra atoms engineers wanted to use. But germanium stopped working if it got too hot.

One reason Jack Kilby had come to work for Texas Instruments was because they had found a way to purify silicon. Silicon, harder to handle, could stand heat. Besides, T.I. had already invested millions of dollars in equipment to process silicon for use in transistors. Jack wondered what else it could do.

He already knew it could be made to conduct electricity. Transistors proved that. Could he also build a resistor out of silicon? Why not? Pure silicon resisted electron movement, almost as well as carbon. In fact, with special doping, it looked as if silicon could be made to do almost anything.

That thought gave Jack a marvelous idea. A totally new idea. Suppose all the parts of a circuit could be made out of silicon. Suppose all the sections of a circuit could be made in one piece!

At first, the idea sounded ridiculous. A silicon circuit looked, Jack told himself, "about as sensible as building a boxcar out of gold; you could probably do it, but why bother?"

And yet, Jack knew germanium and silicon could both conduct and resist electricity and more, reasonably well. That was the point. Semiconductors weren't the best at anything, but they could do *everything*. No one had ever tried to make all the components of a circuit out of the same material, all in one piece.

Jack grabbed his laboratory notebook and started to write. He drew a simple circuit. Then he pictured it carved out on a single thin slice of silicon. Could it work? He had no way to run a test alone.

By the time the staff came back from vacation, Jack had his idea thoroughly mapped out. He showed it to his boss, Willis Adcock, the first morning. "Willis was not as high on it as I was," Jack said later.

It looked expensive. It looked time-consuming. Doping several different areas with several different chemicals would be trouble. Still, it looked possible.

Willis compromised. He didn't want to pull workers off the Micro-Modules contract until he had some proof that Jack's wild idea actually worked. He suggested a test. Could Jack make an all-silicon circuit out of separate pieces of silicon? If he could, would it work?

If so, the director would authorize making one the more expensive way, all on one piece. If not, the idea got junked.

Jack took the challenge. Awkwardly, in his large hands, he took a small piece of pure silicon and shaped it into a resistor. Then he took more silicon, properly doped with two different chemicals, and made a capacitor. He connected the two components into a circuit. He hooked in a battery. Invisible electrons moved through the strange-looking circuit. Current flowed. It worked.

With his boss's blessing—and help—Jack went to work on the far more complicated problem of getting it all together on a single strip. He decided to use germanium instead of silicon for the first trial, to make the doping easier.

Jack designed a circuit to include an *oscillator,* which shifts electrons first one direction and then the other, in tiny pulses of power. He drew a capacitor, a transistor, and three resistors, all to be built into a thin rectangle of germanium no bigger than the top half-inch of a toothpick.

On paper, the circuit looked good. Jack and a small crew of helpers spent the next several months trying to translate Jack's drawing into reality, on their tiny chip of germanium. They glued the chip to a small piece of glass and then to a larger glass sheet, to make it easier to handle. Otherwise, months of work could have been buried under a paper clip.

By September 12, the last tiny component had been "built." The finished micro-circuit could display its action on a test screen something like a small television.

If the circuit worked, green light would ripple across the screen in a wavy line. If it didn't, the screen would stay blank. A small group of spectators gathered around Jack Kilby's lab bench to watch.

Jack connected the battery. He rechecked everything. Then he threw the switch. Everyone stared at the screen, where a wavy green line started to glow. Then, according to T.R. Reid, in *The Chip*, "everyone broke into broad smiles."

Success on the first try. Jack had managed to integrate all the parts of a circuit on a single chip. The first *integrated circuit* was born.

Jack Kilby had discoverd a major clue to the mystery of the numbers barrier, but he couldn't figure out a good way to connect the different parts of the one-piece circuit to each other. A maze of thin gold wiring snaked across the top like an unwanted safety net.

For six months, the team struggled. How could they mass-produce it? How could they simplify the wiring?

Then a rumor swept through the plant. RCA Laboratories, someone said, was developing the same idea. If they wanted the glory of discovery (and the value of the patent) for Jack Kilby and Texas Instruments, they had to hurry.

Streamlining the paperwork, T.I.'s lawyers rushed their design to the United States Patent Office. It wasn't really ready. The crude, handmade circuit worked, but the crew still hadn't found a way to manufacture it or even to solve the wiring problem.

Jack added a note suggesting the chip could eventually be connected by gold wires "laid down" on the surface of the chip. But he didn't know how to do it. That part was still a mystery.

The rumor which stirred Texas Instruments into action was both false and true. RCA didn't have the same idea, but a physicist named Robert Norton Noyce, with a little California firm called Fairchild Semiconductor, did.

Since his favorite model airplane had flown away, lost in the Iowa cornfields, Bob Noyce had been interested in radios. Radios could call back model planes. Radios could send and receive messages from friends. Most of all, radios provided fascinating opportunities for experimenting. Bob "was always trying to figure out how everything worked."

At Grinnell College, in Iowa, a lucky break gave Bob the opportunity to figure out how a transistor worked before most people had ever even heard of one. John Bardeen, one of the inventors of the transistor, had been a classmate of Bob's favorite physics professor, Grant Gale, and he provided his friend's class with two of the very first samples of the new technology.

The "solid state" transistor amazed Bob. "It hit me like the atom bomb," he said. (In 1949, an atom bomb was still new and amazing.) He decided to make a career in transistors.

Eight years later, with a Ph.D. in physics from M.I.T. behind him, Bob Noyce and seven other young physicists and engineers founded Fairchild Semiconductor, in the Santa Clara Valley south of San Francisco. The group rented a two-story warehouse in an apricot orchard. There they began to manufacture transistors—very tiny transistors.

As Bob put it, the working technique involved "making... transistors in a perfect array on a single wafer," of silicon or germanium, and then "cut[ting] them apart into tiny pieces." Then they had to "hire thousands of women with tweezers to pick them up and try to wire them together."

Building transistors turned out to be frustrating work. Continually, they ran into the barrier mystery. Most of the applications they designed for their tiny transistors turned out to be too complicated to build.

No one had any answers. No one was even looking for answers. A different mystery worried them more. How could they get rid of dust?

Dust is deadly to transistors. One tiny speck, embedded in the silicon sheet, can spoil a whole batch. Every day, in their processing rooms, they waged war against the dust from the orchard outside.

Then one of the scientists thought of an idea. What, Jean Hoerni asked, if they baked a protective layer of silicon oxide over the top of every transistor, like a built-on dust cover?

Bob loved the thought of "building a transistor inside a cocoon." They tried it. It worked.

New ideas set people thinking. Bob began to speculate on other ways to use the "planar process," as they named Hoerni's protective layer.

Bob Noyce never liked working alone. He had better luck trying out his sometimes wild ideas on other people. That January, 1959, he spent a lot of time talking about the planar process. He fastened an unblinking stare on his mostly taller co-workers, as he thought out loud. The "cocoon," he kept saying, had to be good for more than just sealing out dust.

One idea came quickly. It wasn't easy, getting thinner-than-a-human-hair wires to stick in exactly the right spots on a fingernail-sized transistor chip. Nor was it easy to get the wires to stay attached.

Bob saw marvelous advantages to the new coating. Wires could poke down through it and even lay down in it, like decorations on a frosted cake. With the silicon oxide layer to hold them still, wires had a much better chance of hitting the right spot and of staying put.

Then the earthshaking idea occurred to Bob. He could print thin metal lines of copper or gold right in the oxide layer, as it was being manufactured. His transistors wouldn't need atttached wires at all.

No wires! But wires and connections, with all the space they took up and with the impossibility of attaching them to super-tiny circuits, were half of what the barrier mystery was about. Without even looking, Bob Noyce had discovered the perfect solution.

Coming at the mystery from a different direction, Bob solved the connections problem first. From there, it was easy to imagine an integrated circuit (very much like the one Jack Kilby had invented six months before). He began drawing pictures in his lab notebook, writing explanations on the side.

For days, Bob wrote suggestions in his notebook. He didn't have to clear them with a boss—he *was* one of the bosses—but he talked every problem over with his colleagues. Finally, on January 23, "all the bits and pieces came together." Bob put together a complete, working integrated circuit with the wiring built in. It worked. The barrier mystery had been solved.

In basic science, ideas are often shared freely. In business, ideas for new products get patented. When two people invent the same thing at almost the same time, the patent race can be messy. Texas Instruments and Fairchild Semiconductor argued and fought for ten years in court over who owned the invention. (The final appeals have still not been settled.)

Robert Noyce won. Jack Kilby had the idea first, but Bob, the court said, had it better. His invisibly wired integrated circuit looked complete. Jack's didn't.

Meanwhile, industry had not waited for the outcome of the ten-year battle. Company after company began manufacturing the versatile new chips by applying for a license from both T.I. and Fairchild. After the court ruled, companies still bought licenses from both. Jack and Bob became known as co-inventors. Jack got credit for the circuit; Bob, for the connections.

When they made their mystery-solving discoveries, Bob Noyce and Jack Kilby had never met or even heard of each other. They were four years apart in age, almost a foot different in height, half a country apart in location, and not even in the same profession: engineer vs. physicist.

Bob, who always liked to "wheel and deal," went on to develop other companies and make millions of dollars in the fast-growing computer industry. He became known as the "Father of Silicon Valley"—which grew up around their northern California apricot orchard.

Jack, who liked to invent things, invented the first hand-held calculator. It made Texas Instruments, where Jack still works, a leader in the field. He also invented a new kind of solar cell, but Jack swears he still doesn't know how to use a computer.

The first microchips went on the market in 1961. They offered about a dozen integrated components, for about $120. Twenty-five years later, chips with more than a million components sold for about five dollars, and operated many times faster. No end seems to be in sight.

The discovery of the integrated circuit opened the Computer Age. Like Madame Curie's discovery of radioactivity, it changed the world forever.

# 11

# UNDERCOVER DRUG DEAL

An addict in New York shoots liquid heroin into a vein in his arm. He begins to feel "high" almost as soon as the drug hits the bloodstream. In a hospital in St. Louis, an accident victim with a fractured leg receives an injection of morphine. Pain relief comes almost instantly. Across the world and centuries ago, an elderly Chinese smoked brown lumps of opium, made from the juice of a blood-red poppy. He felt the same swift rush of pleasure users feel today. But why?

Doctors had been puzzled for years. Why should tiny doses of certain pain-killing, euphoria-producing drugs, made from an opium poppy, work so quickly and so well? It seemed almost as if the molecules of medicine knew exactly where to go—as if the body had been designed to make use of those particular molecules. Researchers Candace Beebe Pert and Solomon Snyder suspected the answer to the mystery lay undercover, deep inside the brain. But where? And how? And why?

For Candace Pert, the mystery started in 1970, in a Texas

hospital. She was the patient, lying prone in bed with a broken back. Days before, she had been thrown from a galloping horse, and the pain from her injury took control of her life. The high points of each day came when a nurse injected small doses of Demerol into her aching body. Almost instantly, the pain stopped. She felt euphorious, wonderful. Candace began to crave the drug.

Underneath the craving, Candace wondered why. Why did the terrible pain stop so quickly? Why should Demerol, made from the same Oriental poppy from which opium comes, feel so good and work so well? And why was her body becoming addicted? The whole drug process was a mystery, and Candace wanted to solve it.

Even before the accident, Candace Beebe Pert had been interested in the brain and how it works. Now, lying in a San Antonio hospital, instead of magazines or novels, Candace read scientific papers on brain chemistry. She planned to enter graduate school at the famous Johns Hopkins laboratories in the fall, and she wanted to be ready. Slowly she recovered from the accident, withdrew from pain-killing drugs, and learned all she could about the brain.

Candace Beebe couldn't have had a less likely start toward scientific detective work. She began college as an English major, changed schools twice, dropped out, took a job as a secretary, married graduate student Agu Pert, had a baby, and worked as a cocktail waitress—all before graduating cum laude with a major in biology from Bryn Mawr, in Pennsylvania, and all in the mid-1960s, when women scientists had a difficult time being taken seriously. The only thing consistently going for Candace all this time was her intelligence. Almost everyone who met her recognized that she was brilliant.

Getting a chance at graduate school took extra effort. Most school administrations thought a woman with a baby ought to stay at home. Pulling all the strings she could, taking advantage of every chance meeting, Candace managed to arrange for herself a spot in the lab of Dr. Solomon Snyder, medical doctor, psychiatrist, and researcher in pharmacology at Johns Hopkins. There, she could get her Ph.D. There, work was already going on toward Candace's pet mystery—drugs and the brain.

Most drugs put into the body don't affect the brain at all. A special "safety net" called the blood-brain barrier screens out almost all kinds of medicines before they can penetrate the brain. A class of drugs called opiates is different. Discovered centuries ago in China and refined and improved by modern scientists, opiates not only get past the blood-brain barrier, they do it with amazing speed. Even the tiniest dose of morphine, codeine, Demerol, or a number of others (heroin is an illegal example) can have a huge effect. Doctors wondered why.

Several clues already pointed toward a possible answer. The brain might have special locations—scientists named them receptor sites—where opiates could attach themselves and get right to work. The researchers pictured a sort of "keyhole" arrangement on the outside of a nerve cell, where opiate molecules could fit like a key into a lock. The idea made sense, but scientists were just guessing.

Other scientists disagreed. Why, they asked, should the body have special receptors for "outside" drugs? Did nature plan for people to use heroin? Put that way, the receptor idea did not make sense. The whole thing was a mystery.

At Hopkins, Candace spent more than a year taking classes

and learning how major laboratories operate. She assisted with other scientists' projects; they found her work "sloppy." She learned to be more careful. Meanwhile, her husband, Agu, a biologist-psychologist and an Army officer stationed at a base twenty-five miles from the lab, learned a lot about housekeeping and child care.

Candace drove daily between the base and Baltimore, besides spending long hours in the lab. She and Agu lived one day at a time. "Very organized," Candace called her life-style.

All through her training, Candace kept the brain-drug mystery in mind. It still fascinated her. In fact, now she knew the specific part of the puzzle she wanted to tackle. Candace Pert wanted to find the opiate receptor. She wanted to locate the "mystery keyholes" where opiate drugs work.

Dr. Solomon Snyder, head of the lab where Candace worked, did, too. He became determined when he heard a lecturer from Stanford University, Dr. Avram Goldstein, describe a method for actually finding opiate receptor cells in the brain. It sounded good. The only problem: so far, no one had been able to make the method actually work. Hints, but no real answers.

Sol Snyder took massive notes on Goldstein's method, adding pages of his own ideas. Thinking through experiments was Sol's specialty. He never did the actual bench work of an experiment, not even when he was in college. "I'm clumsy," Dr. Snyder explains. Besides, "something might explode." Thinking was what he did best. He assigned the laboratory work to Candace Pert.

Candace was more than ready. She had found the simple projects already on her lab bench boring. Candace Pert always hated being bored. She wasn't looking for an easy road to her Ph.D., she wanted to solve a real scientific mystery. Finally, she had the chance.

Candace plunged into the project with enthusiasm. She had already read Dr. Goldstein's book, while lying in the hospital. Now Sol Snyder gave her Goldstein's new article, along with his own notes. She tried the suggested method. It didn't work. She tried a slightly different approach. That didn't work either. She tried all of Snyder's first ideas and some more of her own. Nothing worked.

Candace didn't want to quit. Finally she had found a problem worth solving, and she didn't intend to let go of it. Carefully, she reviewed the clues she had collected so far.

Clue #1: efficiency, the clue she had observed on herself in the hospital. Opiate drugs work quickly and well. That indicated that they may have a specific site to work on.

Clue #2: saturation. If a little morphine works well, a lot should work better. But it doesn't. Beyond a certain point, adding more of an opiate drug has no effect (except to poison). The body seems saturated, as if all the "receptors" are full.

Clue #3: stereochemistry, or the shape of the drug molecules involved. Some molecules, including opiates, are shaped as mirror images of each other, like right- and left-handed gloves. Dr. Goldstein and others had already noticed that, like several other kinds of body chemicals, all opiate drugs are "left-handed." Only the "left-handed" opiates, called levorotatory, have any effect as pain-killers.

"Right-handed," or dextrorotatory opiate molecules—exactly like the others except for the opposing shape—do nothing. Candace could picture this in her mind as trying to force a right mitten onto a left hand. The "receptors" she was looking for had to be "left hands" looking for "left-hand mittens."

Next, Candace reviewed the method she was using. First she had to break a mouse's neck, remove its brain, and "homogenize" the brain tissue with an electric machine something like a cake mixer, into a sort of gray sludgy "milk shake." That was the easy part.

The original idea was to mix an opiate drug with brain tissue, ground up to provide more cell surface area, and measure how much of the drug stuck. Unfortunately, almost everything "stuck." No one could tell what "stuck" where, or why.

Dr. Goldstein had suggested flooding brain tissue with a giant overdose of some opiate drug. Every receptor site should fill up, but drug molecules would also stick to lots of other places on the nerve cells, helter-skelter all over the area, exactly as Candace kept finding.

The next step in Goldstein's plan was to wash the tissue carefully, rinsing away all the excess drug. Only the drug molecules actually locked into receptor sites should remain. Now add more of the same drug, but use a radioactive form. Radioactivity is easy to trace, using a machine called a scintillation counter, which records and counts tiny flashes of light each time a radioactive particle passes through. The amount that sticks is easy to measure. But since all the receptor sites are already full, this will show how much sticks to the mouse brains in other ways. "Nonspecific binding," the researchers called it. Background noise.

Now, start over on fresh mouse brains and flood the tissue with a "right-handed" form of the drug. This should stick everywhere *except* the receptor sites, since the shape of the "key" doesn't fit the "keyhole." Now add the original left-handed drug, made radioactive. Measure how much sticks. Subtract experiment one from experiment two, and you should have receptor site binding. Unfortunately, it didn't work. Candace tried again and again. The results of the two experiments came out pretty much the same.

Candace and Sol Snyder both liked fast, simple experiments best—the kind researchers call "quick and dirty." They favored experiments that started in the morning and showed results by the same afternoon. They got lots of instant results—all negative. No receptor site binding stood out from the general confusion.

Every new idea ended in failure. More than once, Candace gave up. What was the point? She went home to her husband and son, Evan. Then, the next morning or the day after, she thought of a new approach.

Normally a little slapdash, Candace trained herself to use extra care, especially since she was usually working with tiny, two-milliliter amounts—less than a teaspoonful of "mouse brain soup" for each test. Gradually Candace, with input from Sol Snyder, began to make improvements upon the method.

Flooding, they soon realized, was out. It simply made too big a mess. Small doses of drug and then a thorough washing—with eight to ten milliliters of solution, or about a tablespoonful—gave much clearer results. But that also washed away most of the radiation. Sometimes too little to count stayed behind. More failure.

Candace found something stronger. Using a "hot" (strongly radioactive) drug called dihydromorphine, she started all over.

Now, the radiation was much easier to count. Unfortunately, now nothing seemed to be sticking. All the dihydromorphine seemed to wash away. She didn't know the lights of the lab broke down the drug into useless parts. Still more failure.

Candace learned to let the brain-drug mixture stand fifteen minutes, at a temperature close to normal mouse body temperature—then chill it to almost freezing before pouring it into a funnel lined with glass fiber filters. She figured out a way to rinse the ground-up brains under a partial vacuum, using ice-cold solutions, to wash away more of the excess drug.

She sliced cross sections of frozen mouse brain thinner than tissue paper, for examining under a microscope. "I used the hair dryer to dry the slides," she said later. "It's a very useful lab tool." Still, nothing was working.

All this time, Sol Snyder kept a close watch over the project. "I was his pet," Candace says.

"She was more aggressive than the other students... very creative," her boss says. Snyder worried that Candace might be spending too much time on the mystery, when she could be earning her degree some faster way. He thought finding a solution to the brain drug mystery looked like a "million-to-one shot."

For nine or ten months, nothing good happened. Experiment after experiment failed. Then Candace read a paper about opiate antagonists and how they work.

Opiate drugs relieve pain and cause a pleasant, euphoric feeling. Researchers call them "agonists," which means the "leading role in a drama."

Another class of drugs, called antagonists, have the opposite effect—the "opposing role." They seem to displace opiate drugs in the body. An injection of an effective antagonist can bring an overdosed heroin addict back from near death.

Candace stared at chemical sketches of antagonist molecules. Chemically, they looked ridiculously similar to the agonists she already knew about. Most molecules were exactly the same in the "key" section—the part of the molecule that ought to lock into a receptor. But most antagonists had some kind of extra atomic group attached to the other end of the molecule. Usually, but not always, it seemed to "stick out" from the rest of the molecule.

The article didn't explain how the body knows the difference between agonists and antagonists, or how that subtle difference blocks all the pain-killing, euphoria-producing power opiate agonists have. Here was another mystery.

Candace didn't worry about that. One mystery at a time! She got right to the heart of the article. Since antagonists work almost as fast as agonists do, they must work at the same receptor sites. This looked more like a clue than anything Candace had discovered in months. Antagonists seemed to "fit the same keyholes," only instead of unlocking the door, they locked it tighter.

At an Army research center, Candace's husband, Agu Pert, had been working with monkeys, testing their reactions to pain-killing drugs. Morphine relieved pain, but an antagonist drug called naloxone counteracted the effects of morphine. It worked perfectly. A small dose of naloxone neutralized morphine, right inside the monkey's brain, every time, as if no morphine had ever been given.

Candace knew about her husband's work. They talked to each other about mice and monkeys and lab activities whenever they had time to talk. So far, Candace hadn't connected Agu's live monkeys with her own mashed-up mice.

Now, Candace began to think. All along, she had been using opiate agonists—the pain-killers—to try and locate receptor cells. But this paper hinted that opiate antagonists—the antipain-killers—seemed to compete for the same receptors, and do it better! Agu's work hinted at the same thing. Candace knew she had stumbled upon a major clue.

The lab at Johns Hopkins didn't have any naloxone available, but Agu's lab had plenty. He gave her a supply. Unfortunately, the drug the Army was using would not work for Candace's experiments. Her drug had to be radioactive.

Candace agonized over what to do. She knew where to send the drug, to get it made radioactive, but should she? The project had been using up a lot of time and money already, while getting nowhere. Irradiating drugs wasn't cheap. Candace was afraid Solomon Snyder would refuse to okay the extra expense.

Years later, scientists sometimes disagree about parts of the story of their discovery. Candace Pert describes mailing off a sample of naloxone powder to be made radioactive all on her own, without any departmental permission. Solomon Snyder tells about discussing the idea with her and giving his permission.

Whichever way it happened, the sample, now liquid, came back a few weeks later, strongly radioactive. Candace had to dry it, purify it, dry it again, check its purity.... The details seemed to take forever.

On September 22, 1972, Candace added a tiny amount of radioactive naloxone to a minced mouse brain already soaked in an opiate drug. She rinsed the sample and measured how much naloxone "stuck," with the receptors already full.

Then she treated fresh minced mouse brain with radioactive naloxone. The scintillation count was more than twice as high, something like eight hundred counts to two thousand. The radioactive drug almost let her "see" the empty receptor sites filling up. "Experiments either work or they don't work," says Candace. For the first time, this one worked.

The next morning, Candace showed her results to her boss, Sol Snyder. He slowly absorbed the data and then began jumping around the room, screaming and swearing and shouting with glee. The new method turned out positive results the first time. The mystery was almost solved.

Now, things changed around the lab. "Quick and dirty" experiments are great for locating a discovery, but they won't do for pinning down the details. They won't do for sharing results with the world, either.

Snyder realized the need to get all their data in perfect scientific order. He also knew they had to hurry. Modern science is something of a race, with the prizes going to the researcher who announces a discovery first.

He assigned an assistant to Candace, and the two of them, graduate student and technician, set up slower, more carefully planned experiments to confirm the results Candace had found. They organized ways to accomplish those slower experiments as quickly as possible, while Dr. Snyder urged them to hurry.

The method worked, again and again. The team tried rat and guinea pig brains, with the same results. After all the "nonspecific" bonding had been rinsed away, opiate receptors accounted for more than half of the drug activity. Even guinea pig intestines, which scientists already knew react strongly to opiate drugs, had their own receptor sites.

They tried dissecting the tiny rodent brains into different parts, or brain areas, before mashing them. The biggest concentration of opiate receptors lay in the corpus striatum, a part of the brain which regulates motor activity and feeling. Logically, they found fewer receptors in "thinking" areas of the brain.

They tried different drugs. Morphine, codeine, and even methadone, used by former heroin addicts to prevent withdrawal symptoms, each showed a different level of effect. Drugs already known to be strong worked better than weak ones because they "unlocked" more receptors. The stronger the drug, the more it resisted naloxone's effects. Morphine, for instance, worked four times as effectively as methadone, and acted 3,000 times stronger than codeine. (In a living body, the difference is more like ten to one.) In most cases, the drugs reacted just the way doctors would have predicted.

Next they tried other kinds of tissue cells. Candace went through the whole procedure with human blood cells, yeast, and rat's liver. No receptor cells showed up.

As a final check, they tried the same experiment with phenobarbital, a nonopiate pain-killer. Would it attach to the receptor cells? They all held their breath until the results came out of the radiation counter. It didn't stick.

They worked up several other nonopiate drugs. If even one attached to the receptor sites, the whole experiment would fall apart. Not one did. They arranged all their data in neat charts and tables.

Three months later, Candace and her technician had tried every experiment they and Sol Snyder could think of. All the details checked. The team wrote a paper for *Science* magazine, and mailed it in. Candace's name was at the top of the article.

They published their find just in time. Almost simultaneously two other researchers, Lars Terenius of Sweden and Eric Simon of the New York University School of Medicine, announced the same discovery.

The solution to the mystery excited researchers all over the world. Most of all, it uncovered a new mystery—why should the body *have* opiate receptors? Did the body produce opiate-type drugs itself?

Within a few months, other researchers began finding natural pain-killers in the body, which "keyed-in" to opiate receptor sites. They are still finding them, in an on-going mystery chase.

Meanwhile, Dr. Solomon Snyder received the 1978 Lasker Prize for his discovery, along with two other researchers, Dr. John Hughes and Dr. Hans Kosterlitz, of the University of Aberdeen, Scotland, who found the first natural opiatelike drugs in the body. Lasker Prize winners often receive Nobel Prizes, a few years later. Dr. Candace Pert, graduate student at the time of the discovery, wasn't included. Of the two other men named in the award, Kosterlitz was director of his lab, like Solomon Snyder. The other was a young researcher, more like Candace Pert. Frequently, in the scientific world, graduate students are excluded from prizes involving the work they did. Frequently, so are women.

Receptor cells for opiates and other drugs have now been located all over the body, in all sorts of animals, from humans to bears to salmon. The discovery of opiate receptor cells offers a way to study human drug addiction, and it provides a method to test the efficiency of new drugs without trying them on humans. It has opened a whole new field of scientific research.

# 12

# THE SKELETON'S SECRET

When mystery writer Jessica Fletcher stumbles over a dead body in "Murder, She Wrote," she spends the next hour searching for the killer. When anthropologist Don Johanson made a similar find, he took five years solving the mystery—of a tiny skeleton millions of years old.

Dr. Donald Carl Johanson tells the story of the discovery this way:

> "I noticed something lying on the ground partway up the slope. 'That's a bit of a hominid [humanlike] arm,' I said."
>
> "Can't be," said his assistant. "It's too small. Has to be a monkey of some kind."
>
> "I shook my head. 'Hominid.'"
>
> "What makes you so sure?"
>
> "That piece right next to your hand." It was part of a tiny skull.
>
> Adapted from *Lucy, The Beginnings of Humankind*

On the morning of November 24, 1974, Don Johanson woke up feeling lucky. As the American anthropologist in charge of the Hadar expedition, in a part of Ethiopia nicknamed "the Badlands," Don had planned to spend that Sunday morning catching up on the paperwork stacked in his tent.

Then Tom Gray, graduate student, sat down with Don at breakfast. They talked about the site, marked off into carefully numbered locations. Tom was scheduled to chart location #162, four miles from camp, and he didn't know where it was.

Don decided to show him. The two men drove out in a Land Rover, over rutted, rocky ground. They found site #162, and they also found the most exciting mystery skeleton in the history of anthropology—sticking up out of the dry, eroded sand.

Besides an arm bone and partial skull, Don and Tom saw fragments of ribs, a leg bone, and part of a pelvis lying half-buried in the gravel. They were careful not to disturb the evidence, just like detectives at the scene of a modern murder. They took only a couple of loose bits of skull, carefully marking their location. Then they drove back for help.

The atmosphere around camp crackled with excitement. The scientists celebrated by roasting a goat and cooling beer in the dirty Awash River.

Then the work began. Three weeks of searching, gravel washing, dirt sifting, and digging with tools the size of dental instruments located over a hundred fragments of an ancient female skeleton. Someone in the camp named her "Lucy," after the Beatles hit "Lucy in the Sky with Diamonds." Her official name: AL 288-1, Hadar collection.

The thorough search also turned up fossilized crocodile eggs and crab claws and bones of ancient pigs. Some or all of those might have been Lucy's lunch.

Most anthropological discoveries consist of a few teeth or bits of skull. When all the pieces of Lucy lay assembled on a table, they formed about 40 percent of her whole skeleton. No fossil (bone turned to rock) of a humanlike creature so old and so complete had ever been found before. And so tiny! Lucy's whole head was about the size of a softball.

But who *was* Lucy? More important, *what* was Lucy? Was she human? Was she some ancient kind of ape? She didn't look quite like any specimen the anthropologists had ever seen before.

The scientists could almost picture her living body, as the bones lay on the table. The shape of the pelvis said adult female, but Lucy was only about three-and-a-half feet tall and would have weighed about sixty pounds.

Her bones were thicker than a modern human so short would have, and her arms hung almost as long as a chimpanzee's, but her structure showed that she walked upright, on two legs. Her hands appeared human, except for the slightly curling fingers. Her wrists looked more like those of an ape. Lucy had a flat face and a jutting, vee-shaped lower jaw, but her back teeth looked small and humanlike—and more primitive than any Don Johanson had ever seen.

Lucy was a mystery. Her discoverer needed clues.

Don started searching. First, he needed to know her age. He called in some new "detectives."

Earthquakes and volcano eruptions over billions of years have buckled the hot, dry Afar Valley into dozens of exposed layers called strata. Raging floods blend the strata and wash them away.

Maurice Taieb, the French geologist with the expedition, had been trying to match layers of earth across one gully to another, like sections of a gigantic 3-D picture puzzle. He charted the layers of dirt onto an up-and-down map called a stratigraphic column. On it, he found the first clue. Taieb found a layer of basalt rock, from an ancient volcano flow east of Hadar, which seemed to "fit" several layers below the spot where Lucy lay.

Volcano eruptions can be dated. He and Don guessed this one at roughly three million years, making Lucy a few hundred thousand years younger. Clue #1—questionable.

Then a new investigator arrived, geologist Jim Aronson, from the United States. Jim's careful searching found evidence Taieb had missed—chunks of the basalt had fallen into a river channel, which Taieb had "placed" in the wrong layer. The basalt stratum really belonged much lower on his chart, adding to its—and Lucy's—age. Clue #2—another guess.

Next stop, Case Western Reserve University, in Cleveland, where both Don Johanson and Jim Aronson worked as professors. Jim had invented a machine which might help uncover a more dependable clue to Lucy's age.

The potassium-argon testing machine Jim showed Don had dials and wires and switches and tubes enough to fill a room. "Small," Jim called it. The machine was best, he warned, "at measuring very young things."

"Young things?"

"Only two or three million years old." To a geologist—used to dealing in billions of years—three million is young.

Jim explained the technique. Potassium is a common element, found almost everywhere. A tiny part of it is always radioactive.

Since the world began, radioactive potassium has been slowly decaying into a gas called argon. Right now, potassium atoms in every human body are turning into argon at the rate of 500 every second. They are decaying in rocks, too, and in every material which has potassium. The argon can be measured and used to calculate the age of a potassium-rich material.

Bones let argon leak right out, but the colorless gas collects in volcanic ash and rocks. As radioactive potassium decays, atoms of argon get trapped inside the rocks.

Rocks get banged and battered into sand over millions of years. At Hadar, Jim had collected a box of the least-battered basalt samples he could locate, some from a pale yellow layer just above the strata where Lucy had been found and some from a much lower layer of shiny black sand. Then he had picked up a few samples from a grayish, sugary-textured section of the black strata, storing them in a separate box.

Jim melted the "best" sandy rocks inside his machine and measured the tiny bubbles of argon floating off. Each yellow sample pointed to a similar date—right around 2.6 million years ago. The lower, black strata calculated to a date of around 3.0 million. The results looked good, but Aronson was suspicious.

All the tiny rocks had tiny broken spots. Had they leaked?

For a check, Jim melted some of his "gray sugar" rocks. They tested thousands of years younger than the black samples, even though Jim knew their age had to be the same. He suspected that every rock in his collection had probably lost some argon. Losing argon makes a sample read younger than it really is.

Jim's safest estimate said the rock layer around Lucy had to be "a minimum" of three million years old. Clue #3: suspicious.

Then Jim thought of another possible clue. Geologists know something most people don't. The North Pole has not always been positive and the South Pole negative as they are today. Sometimes they switch polarity, or "flip-flop," in a way that would make compasses point south instead of north. A precise geologic chart plots exactly when each global "flip-flop" occurred, stretching back millions of years.

Tom Schmitt, a Cleveland geologist, collected four hundred rock samples from Hadar, arranging them from youngest to oldest. Then he checked the magnetic crystals inside.

Most volcanic rocks from the black, basalt layer of the Hadar site showed reverse polarity. That meant North and South had been reversed when the volcano which created that layer blew. As the super-hot lava cooled into rocks, magnetism froze like a fingerprint, pointing in a reverse direction.

According to the chart, the layer of rock and ash under Lucy's level must have formed between 3.0 and 3.1 million years ago *or* between 3.4 to 3.8 million years ago—two periods when the earth's poles were reversed. In between, and for long periods before and after, the earth was "normal."

The first "flip-flop" period, called the "Mammouth," fit Don's data best. But Jim thought the second period, the "Gilbert," was likelier. A "hunch," he said. Clue #4: confusing.

The next fall, 1975, another expedition left for Hadar. Don Johanson, Jim Aronson, and Tom Gray all joined the group, and Jim took along an assistant, Bob Walter.

The leaders hoped Bob, a volcano expert, might find some new clues to the age mystery. Right away, he did.

Bob Walter traced three thin layers of volcanic ash, in a level known to be "younger" than Lucy. He carefully scooped samples of fine black and white and yellow ash from the middle, least contaminated layer and took them back to the United States, for a new kind of analysis: fission-track dating.

Fission-track dating also involves radioactive atoms changing from one kind into another, but it is completely different from the potassium-argon technique. Uranium-238 slowly decays into lead, with a half-life (the time it takes half a sample to turn to lead) of 4.5 billion years. As each individual atom decays, it gives off a tiny "puff" of energy.

Another dating "detective," took over. C.W. Naser, a geologist from Colorado, cleaned and dissolved and purified the volcanic ash samples until only the heaviest bits of super-fine sand were left. These reddish, powdery grains, he knew from experience, would be tiny zircons, with some uranium mixed in. They ranged in size from about 30 to 120 micrometers (millionths of a meter) across. He carefully spread out eleven of the largest pale red crystals in a layer, one crystal deep, and glued them to a small, flat dish. Then he polished the surface, to remove stray scratches.

As atoms of uranium-238 decay, the energy they give off causes a tiny ripple, or "track" in the crystal, like footprints in wet sand. Naser painted on a chemical to enlarge the marks. Finally, using a high-power microscope, he carefully counted the fission tracks hidden in his tiny gems.

The number of scratches in each crystal gave the geologist a good idea of the age of the ash. He settled upon 2.58 million years as the best answer. Lucy had to be older than 2.58 million years. But how much older? Clue #5: incomplete.

So far, four dating methods had gotten essentially nowhere.

Don could prove Lucy was close to three million years old, but he, like Jim, suspected she was older. Now what?

He was also getting nowhere on the rest of the mystery. Just what was Lucy? Where did she fit into the overall anthropological picture?

Lucy's bones totalled only a small fraction of the hominid fossils discovered at Hadar. The year before, Don had found a knee joint just Lucy's size. Just a month before Lucy turned up, a worker had discovered parts of four partially broken jaw bones with teeth. These jaws were different in shape and much larger than Lucy's tiny face.

The next fall, Don and his group found more mysterious bones at Hadar. Discovered much the same way as Lucy, fossilized bones from at least thirteen individuals, who seem to have died together, turned up spread across a flood-washed gulley and buried in the side of a hill. They included fossils from babies, children, and adults of both sexes, although no individual was nearly as complete as Lucy.

All those bones had to be cleaned and measured, photographed and cast in plaster before the real detective work could start. That process took more than two years.

By mid-1977, Don had crates of mysterious fossils to explain. How did they all relate? He was an expert on jaws and teeth, so he decided to concentrate on those.

Don spread his whole jaw collection, some real bones and some copies, some almost whole and some only fragments, out on a countertop in his basement lab. He stared at the gray teeth and the tea-brown bones. What did they all mean?

Every kind of plant or animal, alive or extinct, has a two-part scientific name. Modern humans are known as *Homo sapiens*.

*Sapiens* is the species name, including all human races alive today. *Homo* is the broader, genus name, including all prehistoric humans as well as modern people.

Some other human species, living mostly one or two million years ago, have been named *Homo erectus* and *Homo habilis*. Anthropologists use "*Australopithecus*" as the genus name for prehumans—extinct creatures which had some humanlike and some apelike characteristics.

The bones scientists collect don't come with their scientific names attached. Anthropologists have to figure them out. Staring at the huge, still-mysterious spread of bones in front of him, Don Johanson wondered where to start.

He started where most modern scientists do. He called in help. Tim White, a graduate student just finishing his doctorate, had already done some anthropological "detective work" on a smaller fossil collection from another African expedition, about a thousand miles from Hadar. Don invited him to work on the mystery.

Tim brought plaster casts of the fossils from Laetoli, Tanzania, with him. Those bones had been dated at close to four million years old. Between them, they had bits and pieces of at least thirty-five and perhaps as many as sixty-five different individuals. The two spread all their jaw and tooth fragments out on the same countertop.

Both men immediately noticed a clue: the two sets looked amazingly alike. For samples discovered a thousand miles and at least a quarter of a million years apart, the jaws all appeared to be part of the same collection.

Except for Lucy. Lucy's tiny vee-shaped jaw looked different. The mystery seemed to be a double-header—Lucy, and all the rest.

Tim didn't agree. Lucy was definitely female. Sometimes the female of a species is much smaller. In apes, even the proportional sizes of male and female teeth are very different. What if the biggest jaws were all male? What if Lucy just happened to be especially short?

Don disagreed. In fact, the two men argued, their voices loud in the cavernous basement.

Don pointed to the vee-shape of Lucy's jaw. Definitely some kind of odd-looking *Australopithecus*. The jaws of the others were rounder and more human-looking—like the genus scientists call *Homo*. Don remembered an interview he gave a *Time* magazine reporter about one set of jaws. "I recognized the fossil almost at once as one of the oldest human remains ever discovered," Don had been quoted in *Time*.

In fact, Don had recently appeared at a news conference, describing his fossils (all but Lucy) as "what an early form of *Homo* may have been like." He had told *everybody* he thought they were human. Now he was supposed to lump them in the same grouping with prehuman Lucy? No way!

Tim and Don agreed on only one thing. They needed more clues. They needed a new way to attack the mystery.

Searching for a method, the two found a years-old study comparing, point by point, the jaws of australopithecines to both apes and humans. That gave them the framework they needed. They decided to compare their fossils, point by point, to all three.

At night, when the lab was empty and quiet (except for the hooting of caged owls in the lab next door), Don and Tim started the search. They began to examine each bone, individually, feature by feature.

The first new clue startled both men. Their fossils turned out to be more apelike than any other hominids known. "Instead of being human with apish tendencies," Don said, "they seemed more apish with human tendencies."

Apes have boxy jaws, with straight sides. Human jaws are rounded. The fossil jaws looked like rounded boxes. The Hadar skulls had low flat palates, as apes do, and they had apelike faces, with tiny brains and swollen, apelike canine tooth roots.

And yet, the two researchers kept finding humanlike clues. All the jaws, including Lucy, had relatively small back teeth, like modern humans. More like modern humans, in fact, than any australopithecines known. Some of the body bones could have been mistaken for a small, modern human. The clues seemed to be pointing in two different directions at once.

Anthropologists believe that, over millions and millions of years, apelike ancestors developed into well-known forms of australopithecines which finally developed into humans. These fossils didn't fit the usual picture at all. They had to be, Tim and Don agreed, something new. But what? And how many? One new thing or two?

Here, Tim and Don started arguing, again. Tim said one. Don said two. He was convinced Lucy had to be something different. Hadn't he already said so, in print, a dozen times?

The windowless lab had shelves along the wall, holding box after box of classified bones. Don and Tim compared their samples, one-on-one, with literally hundreds of other bones—human and chimpanzee and australopithecine. In every case, they found the same mysterious results. Their fossils looked more apish *and* more human then any other prehuman, both at the same time.

Then Tim lined up a carefully chosen sample of their fossil skull parts and molds on the counter, arranging them in order of size from the biggest ones right down to Lucy. Suddenly, Don saw something he had never noticed before.

Lucy didn't look much like the large skulls at the head of the line, but she looked very much like those nearest her in size. Those, in turn, looked very much like the next larger set, and so on. The graduated order of size suddenly made everything clear.

Lucy had the same teeth, the same basic shape, the same *everything* as the other skulls, only in miniature. Lucy belonged to the set, right at the end of the line—except for one problem. Lucy still had that sharp, vee-shaped jaw no other skull in the series had.

Solving the final argument took only pencil and paper, and the rest of one evening. When the other jaws in the series were scaled down, on paper, to the smaller size of Lucy, their slightly pointed jaws became vee-shaped, too. Simple arithmetic proved that Lucy's jaw shape came from the size of her tiny teeth, not from a major difference in species. Don had, he realized, been wrong all along.

Their conclusions: the hominid fossils from Hadar and Laetoli, including Lucy, represented one species—a new species of prehuman older than any other known. They named Lucy and the whole collection *Australopithecus afarensis*, from the Afar Valley, where most of the bones were discovered. Most (but not all) anthropologists now accept the new species as fact.

The rest of their solution to the mystery is still speculation. From the evidence they had, Don Johanson and Tim White placed *A. afarensis* at the very top of the evolutionary chart.

That species, they decided, developed into other lines of australopithecines, which then became extinct, *and* into all lines of modern humans. That theory explained the apelike as well as the humanlike characteristics.

Meanwhile, the final clue to the dating puzzle landed neatly in place, provided by a collection of pigs. Since the same kind of pigs seemed to live at the same time in all parts of Africa, pig bones can be used as a time-line. A team of scientists concocted a chart of pig fossils similar to the stratigraphic map geologists use. The system is called "biostratigraphy."

Finished in 1978, the pig chart placed Don Johanson's collection of fossils at older than three million years, or straight in the "Gilbert" magnetic period. The final date selected for Lucy's life and death is 3.5 million years ago.

In anthropology, very few mysteries are ever permanently solved. New evidence may change the whole picture. But whatever happens, Lucy, herself, has solved one old mystery indisputably. Lucy walked upright on two legs, as modern humans do, three-and-a-half-million years ago. Before Lucy, scientists could only guess how prehumans moved, so far in the past. Now that much, at least, they know for sure.

# 13
# THE CASE OF THE COLD CONDUCTOR

In a classic "locked room" mystery, the crime takes place in a room sealed from the inside. The criminal vanishes, leaving only his victim behind.

In a famous "locked room" mystery, Dutch scientists tracked a well-known "thief" to the scene of a "crime"—when the "thief" suddenly vanished from inside a sealed bottle. Even more mysterious, nothing else was missing. They had expected electricity to disappear.

Every time electrical energy travels through a wire, as much as 40 percent of it may be "stolen" along the way. Metal wires resist carrying energy, and that *resistance*—the well-known "thief"—steals electricity by turning it into heat. Power companies lose billions of dollars worth of electricity to resistance every year.

How to stop the loss is a worldwide mystery. Most scientists thought it could never be solved—until some startling new discoveries "caught the scientific community," says *Chemical &*

*Engineering News*, May 11, 1987 issue, "totally off-guard." They revitalized the old, on-going case.

1911, University of Leiden, Holland: The first clue turned up accidentally, seventy-five years ago. Physicist Heike Kamerlingh Onnes had designed an elaborate laboratory for low-temperature work, where he had just managed to liquify helium gas at the amazingly low temperature of 452 *degrees below zero, Fahrenheit.*

Helium, which some scientists had thought could never be liquified, is the gas used in lighter-than-air balloons. Heike Kamerlingh Onnes got a Nobel Prize for his efforts.

Now, Kamerlingh Onnes had a way to keep things super-cold. He could dip them in liquid helium. He began using the frigid liquid to study other materials at low temperatures. He found a mystery.

The Dutch scientists had graphed the behavior of helium and other gases at lower and lower temperatures, to see what happened. The graphs led them to a temperature called *absolute zero*, where no heat existed. All graphs pointed to the same lowest possible temperature— -459.67° Fahrenheit, or -273.15° Celsius. The point became "zero" on a new scale— the Kelvin scale, which has units (not followed by a degree sign) the same size as Celsius degrees.

The next set of graphs uncovered a puzzle. Scientists thought metals would conduct electricity better and better, as temperatures dropped down toward 0° K. Then they would turn into insulators. When electrons became cold enough, the physicists reasoned, they would stop moving. Conductance would halt completely.

That didn't happen. Not even close. A graduate student

dipping a sample of mercury into liquid helium, found exactly the opposite. Current passed through the metal like magic, with no loss at all. Resistance vanished completely. Kamerlingh Onnes was so surprised, as the story goes, "he fell out of his lab chair."

More experiments confirmed the mysterious result. The mercury, chilled to almost absolute zero, had lost all resistance to electricity. The same thing happened to tin and lead, each at a different super-low temperature. The Dutch physicists named their unexpected discovery "supra-conductivity." (Later, the spelling changed to "super.")

No one wanted to believe the mysterious find. Electrical current *had* to lose energy while passing through a wire. Physics theories demanded it.

Kamerlingh Onnes sent a superconducting metal ring, immersed in a thermos flask filled with liquid helium, all the way from Holland to London as proof. When the skeptical British scientists tested the tiny ring, it still carried as much current as the Dutch scientists had started in it, weeks before.

Electricity is a stream of electrons. In a normal conductor, electrons bump into atoms and each other in the framework of the materials they pass through, like a marcher going the wrong way in a parade. Current disappears.

In a superconductor, on the other hand, the framework actually seems to help electrons along, like a star athlete riding on the shoulders of the team. Current lasts.

The theory explaining superconductivity is complex and possibly outdated. One point matters: The moving electrons have their energy lowered so much that they cannot, due to the quantum theory (see "The Curious Quantum Mystery"), give up any more. Since they can't lose any energy, they sail around and around the metal with no resistance, no formation of heat, and no loss of current. Current lasts forever.

Scientists hoped superconductivity could solve the mystery of disappearing electricity. They tried all the different elements. Only about two dozen turned out to be superconducting, each at a "critical temperature," $T_c$, lower than about 10 K (-422°F). They tried different alloys, or mixtures of metals. The $T_c$ of the best stuck at 23 K.

To work, superconductors had to be kept hundreds of degrees colder than the coldest day in Antarctica. Each superconductor had to be surrounded by expensive liquid helium, the only refrigerant cold enough. Using superconductivity almost always cost more than it saved.

To solve the mystery, scientists knew a superconductor needed to work at a temperature at least as high as liquid nitrogen, the refrigerant used in grocery freezer trucks. Nitrogen, much cheaper than helium, boils at 77 K. Getting superconductivity up that high looked like an impossible dream. Most physicists quit trying.

1973: Several researchers discovered, to their surprise, that some *oxides*—compounds of metal and oxygen—could become superconducting. No one had ever tried oxides before. Normally, oxides don't conduct electricity at all.

This discovery was a major clue to the mystery, but almost no one noticed. Oxide research faded away.

1982, University of California, Berkeley: Physics professor Marvin L. Cohen found another clue. By feeding their giant computer data about different materials, Cohen's team developed a program to predict when (or if) those materials might become superconducting. But were the predictions true? No one knew.

1983: Researchers in France tested some of the California predictions. They discovered a material made of silicon, the main ingredient of sand, which became superconducting at 440 degrees below zero Fahrenheit, *while under more than two million pounds per square inch pressure.* The discovery was not too useful—many metals already superconduct more easily than that—but it proved the computer right. One more clue to the mystery.

1983, I.B.M. Zurich Research Center, Switzerland: J. Georg Bednorz, crystallographer, was working with a special class of metal oxide crystals when a physicist co-worker had an idea. Why, asked K. Alexander Muller, wouldn't the crystals make good superconductors? They had an open microscopic framework, with room for electrons to move. Why not?

Together, the two men ground and mixed and baked and chilled a variety of oxide crystals, using different combinations of atoms, and then Bednorz and Muller tested the crystals' conductivity. No luck. They kept trying.

1985, University of Caen, France: French chemists Claude Michel and Bernard Raveau had been doing research on crystals combining four elements—lanthanum, barium, copper, and oxygen. They had never bothered to test for superconductivity.

January, 1986, Zurich: The French team's new oxide, which looked like a dark chunk of pottery, seemed just the clue the I.B.M. researchers had been hunting. They set up their apparatus, and on January 27 Muller passed a current through the new substance. All resistance to electricity dropped suddenly at a $T_C$ of 35 K. No one had ever found superconductivity at a temperature so "high" (room temperature is about 300 K)! Finally, after three years of failure, a new clue.

More experiments needed doing, but the Swiss team didn't have the right equipment. They sent their early data to a German physics magazine, set for publication a few months later. Until then, they kept the discovery secret.

They needn't have bothered. When the article was published, few scientists paid much attention. In fact, almost no one believed them.

Almost no one. Two laboratory directors, on opposite sides of the world, took the Swiss discovery seriously. In Tokyo and in Texas, new efforts began....

October, 1986, Switzerland: Bednorz and Muller finally located the magnetic equipment they needed. With help from an associate visiting from Japan, they announced a special confirmation of their own discovery.

Besides dropping all resistance to electricity, a true superconductor has a second effect. It pushes magnetic lines out and away from itself. Called the Meissner effect, the pushing action happens at the exact moment a material becomes superconducting.

The I.B.M. team at Zurich measured the magnetic lines in their sample. The lines had disappeared, but only from part of the oxide. Their discovery seemed to be only partially superconducting. Meanwhile, other scientific teams jumped into the mystery.

November, 1986, University of Tokyo: Shoji Tanaka and a team of scientists confirmed the Swiss experiment. They made a few improvements.

November, 1986, University of Houston, Texas: Ching-Wu (Paul) Chu and his team also confirmed the Swiss experiment. It looked like an amazing clue. Paul Chu decided to solve the rest of the mystery. He wanted to locate or build a real "warm" superconductor—one that could be used anywhere.

Born and raised in China, Paul came to the United States for graduate school, earned his Ph.D. in physics, became an American, and stayed to do research. Dr. Chu had already worked with low-temperature superconductors, he had studied magnets, and he was an expert at applying new and different materials. Now, he began collecting clues from all those fields.

First, Paul Chu noticed the new Swiss ceramic material was not the same compositon in all spots. In fact, it formed layers, like a sandwich. Some layers seemed to superconduct; others didn't.

What kind of changes would improve it? Chu tried replacing barium with strontium, a smaller atom in the same family of elements. The team pushed $T_C$ up to 40 K.

So did Tokyo. By now, more than one hundred laboratories across the world, from New Jersey to the Far East, were experimenting with the mysterious new materials.

January, 1987, Institute of Physics of the Academia, Beijing, China: Using similar materials and working with borrowed equipment in an unheated building, the Chinese team found superconductivity at a new, slightly higher temperature. Unfortunately, their samples fell apart when exposed to air.

X-ray pictures of the superconducting oxides in France, Japan, and the United States all showed one clue in common. They had a mysterious structure called a perovskite, named for a Russian mineral which was named for a Russian Count. The mineral, a yellow-brown calcium and rare earth oxide, forms layers of four-sided crystals. Natural perovskites always have three oxygen atoms for every two of metal, attached at the crystal's corners.

The superconducting perovskites showed differences. Mostly green or black, they had three four-sided, layered crystals built around atoms of copper. Instead of calcium, these contained barium, a similar but much bigger atom.

For the rare earth ingredient, they all used lanthanum. ("Rare earths" is the name given to a group of seventeen not-so-rare but very similar metallic elements.) Most important, for some mysterious reason, about a quarter of the usual oxygen atoms seemed to be missing.

Researchers at Houston, Zurich, and Tokyo had all found the same thing, with minor differences. So had other labs. Making the new layered materials was simple and cheap enough that any lab "with a mortar and pestle and an oven" could do it, one magazine reported. Like "baking brownies," said another. The race for new clues was on.

January, 1987, Houston: Paul Chu read about dozens of unsuccessful tries at superconductivity. He and his co-workers tried a new idea, combining two earlier clues.

The Swiss team had experimented with a new kind of perovskite. Earlier, French researchers had put their sample under heavy pressure. What if someone tried both at the same time?

First, the Houston group heated a mixture of lanthanum oxide, cupric (copper) oxide, and barium carbonate, for four hours. They ground it into powder and then heated it eight more hours. They pressed tiny scoops of the material into tinier pellets and baked them for a day and a half, at varying temperatures and pressures.

Then the team cut off a piece of the brittle pellet, 1 x 1 x 3 millimeters (smaller than the average broken pencil lead) in size. Attaching wires made out of platinum with a paste made out of gold, they began testing for superconductivity under pressure.

The new idea worked. Using thousands of pounds of pressure at hundreds of degrees below zero Fahrenheit, Paul Chu and the Houston team found what *Science* magazine called a "dramatic" result. $T_C$ slid upward, from super-supercold to merely supercold—about 52 K. Another clue.

Superconductivity at 52 K passed all predictions ever made. Chu could not explain why his experiment worked—only that it did. Scientists began calling the use of high pressure on superconductors the "Chu effect."

Soon all the labs could do what the Houston crew did. Meanwhile, they all played around with the chemistry of their samples. The tried pressure. It sometimes helped. They tried replacing barium with strontium. That also helped. Then they tried replacing strontium with calcium (smaller still). That pushed $T_C$ in the wrong direction. They kept trying.

January 17, Beijing: The Chinese team reported some confusing results. They had discovered a surprising $T_C$ of 70 K in one isolated sample. The sample, using some new and different elements, had unstable layers. The Chinese scientists could not quite decide what was happening.

January 29, 1987, Houston: Paul Chu and his team kept on reading every paper they could find on the subject. They didn't want to miss a vital clue. They read about the Chinese puzzle.

Meanwhile, Paul had a new thought. Putting each sample

under pressure—the Chu effect—only pointed to an answer. What was needed, Paul Chu realized, was pressure from within. Somehow, the material needed to constrict itself.

The confusing Chinese results gave him a fresh idea. He began to try some different elements. One combination on his list of possibilities mixed the usual gritty black cupric oxide and white, powdery barium carbonate with a new yellowish-white rare earth powder, yttrium oxide. They ground all three together and baked the new mixture into a dark green chunk.

Paul Chu had combined forces with a friend and former student of his at the University of Alabama-Huntsville. Mau-kuen Wu, experimenting with the new greenish oxide, dropped a tiny crystalline chip into an open insulated flask. Then his team covered it with liquid nitrogen. Wu "knew" nitrogen's boiling point, 77 K, was too high for superconducting, so he didn't expect any surprises as he sent a surge of electricity through the chip.

He got one, anyway. The resistance suddenly dropped to nothing. The chip began to superconduct.

The Alabama scientists supposed they had made a mistake. They tried it again. Same result. "Our hands were shaking" with nervousness, Wu said later.

He contacted Paul Chu in Houston right away. Wu and two assistants flew to Texas.

Then, as *Chemical & Engineering News* reports, the Houston crew "hit the jackpot"! Using the same new material, they found superconductivity beginning at the absolutely astounding $T_C$ of 98 K—far higher than the 77 K boiling point of liquid nitrogen. Magnetic lines disappeared. Every test agreed.

Chu's group knew they had found, not just a slightly better crystal than the last time, but something totally new. Paul called the discovery "a previously unknown phenomenon in physics"—a phenomenon not yet explained.

Paul Chu and the two-state research team had developed a new, porous, perovskite-type metallic oxide very similar to the kind of crystals found in rocks and dirt all over the earth. But Paul's crystal was special. Every test showed just how special it was. "It's really amazing," he told reporters later.

For one thing, chemists had trouble pinning down the structure exactly, because the number of oxygen atoms varied from place to place. The "holes" left by missing oxygen atoms seemed to be an important aid to superconductivity.

Tests show that copper is the most important, most irreplaceable element besides oxygen in the sample. Copper is one of the best ordinary conductors of electricity. But on its own, copper does not superconduct. Nor do any of the other ingredients.

The scientists weren't surprised. It's the mixture, they knew, that matters.

Examining the hard crystals under a microscope showed distinct green and black layers, liked stacked club sandwiches. Other techniques showed odd-shaped "dimples" (like curling bacon) in some of the layers, with copper compounds like "toothpicks" lacing them together.

In some mysterious way not totally understood, the structure "scrunches" itself, applying pressure from inside—just the way Paul Chu had envisioned. No outside pressure turned out to be necessary.

The crystals no longer looked exactly like perovskites. No

natural mineral alternates layers quite the way Paul Chu's crystal does. Somehow, the large barium atom, the mid-sized yttrium atom and the small copper atom hold tightly together, surrounded by atoms of still-smaller oxygen.

Only the black layer, $YBa_2 Cu_3 Ox$, (where x stands for 6 or 7) turned out to superconduct. No one on the team could quite explain why it could superconduct so well—or at all. At that point, no one cared. The main mystery, as far as they were concerned, was solved.

February 16, Houston: The team announced their discovery to the world, but they kept the crystal's composition a secret. Their article describing it was already sitting at a science magazine called *Physical Review Letters*, due out March 2, 1987, and they decided not to "scoop" their own story.

Secrets tend to leak, even with the best efforts. Within days, dozens of labs picked up a rumor. Some started work on the "secret ceramic." The joke was on them. Somehow, Paul Chu's paper contained one small error.

Due to a typographical mistake (some people think it was clever planning), every Y in the manuscript became Yb. Y is the chemical symbol for yttrium—the rare earth Chu used in his superconducting crystal. Yb stands for ytterbium, an entirely different rare earth with a larger atom. Since Chu never spelled out the word, some labs put hours of effort into making ytterbium oxide crystals. They didn't work.

The team in China had been working with the same clues, already. They duplicated the Houston results before the article came out. Immediately afterward, so did groups in Japan, California, and New Jersey. It's "as if Mt. Everest had just been climbed," one of the scientists told *U.S.A. Today.*

Nonscientists didn't care about exact chemical formulas,

anyway. This was the first most people had heard about a weird phenomenon called "superconductivity." They wanted to know what it could do. What does this "solved mystery" really mean?

"I think it could almost be like the discovery of electricity," Paul Chu told *Time* magazine. Other physicists compare it to the invention of the light bulb or the computer chip.

Immediate uses for superconductivity might be faster computers, "waste-free" power lines, better electric motors, giant magnets, and new magnetic detectors to locate submarines. Next, levitating trains, floating at 300 miles per hour on a five-inch-thick cushion of air. Scientists even foresee levitating cars. Eventually, who knows?

Tiny superconducting body probes will give doctors new information. Giant atom-smashers such as Fermilab's Tevatron in Illinois, and CERN in Europe (both already using "old-fashioned" superconduction) may get stronger. The U.S. super-collider now in the planning stages, might save billions of dollars in building and operating costs.

Before the new superconductors can start "working miracles," three more mysteries must be solved. The amount of current they can carry must be raised, they have to work with high magnetic fields, and they need to be formed into wires and other useful shapes. I.B.M., A.T.&T. Bell, and other labs have already had some success with all three problems. Scientists around the world are looking for fresh clues.

I.B.M. is already "painting" the new copper oxides onto chips and circuit boards. Japan is designing trains. Major projects may be only five or ten years away.

Meanwhile, superconducting temperatures are still climbing.

In May, 1987, Paul Chu announced he had found superconductivity in a new material only 54 degrees below zero, Fahrenheit—in the area where dry ice is enough to keep the materials cold. Or "open your window in Alaska," one physicist joked in the *New York Times*. Superconductors at room temperature no longer seem so impossible.

The solution to the Cold Conductor mystery is too new for many prizes or awards or even patents, but something scientists like almost as much—grants of money for more research—is moving fast. Japan is supporting a hurry-up program. In the United States, so is the National Science Foundation and the Department of Energy. Industry and governments everywhere are getting involved.

Some of the new technology may be beyond what anyone can now imagine, but the idea's importance earned Georg Bednorz and Alex Mueller the 1987 Nobel Prize in physics. As other scientific discoveries have done before, superconductivity may change the world.

# INDEX